SAINT KATERI

SAINT KATERI

LILY OF THE MOHAWKS

By
Matthew E. Bunson
and
Margaret R. Bunson

ISBN: 978-1-59276-791-5 (Inventory No. T1096)

eISBN: 978-1-61278-264-5

LCCN: 2012944340

Cover design: Lindsey Riesen

Cover art: "Holding on to Faith," by Nellie Edwards, ImmaculataArt.com

Interior design: Dianne Nelson

PRINTED IN THE UNITED STATES OF AMERICA

*This book is dedicated to the memory of
Margaret R. Bunson (1930-2012),
who passed to her reward as this book
was being completed.*

*"I am no longer my own.
I have given myself entirely to Jesus Christ."*

— Saint Kateri Tekakwitha

CONTENTS

PART ONE:
THE WORLDS OF SAINT KATERI

PART TWO:
THE LIFE OF SAINT KATERI

ACKNOWLEDGMENTS

There are a number of people to whom a debt of gratitude is owed for their kind assistance in the preparation of this manuscript: His Excellency, Most Reverend Charles Chaput, O.F.M. Cap., Archbishop of Philadelphia; Rev. Paolo Molinari, S.J., postulator for the cause of canonization of St. Kateri; Rev. Wayne Paysse, director of the Bureau of Catholic Indian Missions; Patricia O'Rourke; Jane Cavolina; York Young, managing editor of Our Sunday Visitor; Jackie Lindsey, acquisitions editor of Our Sunday Visitor; and Greg Erlandson, president of Our Sunday Visitor. Special thanks are owed to Msgr. Paul Lenz, P.A., for his many decades of friendship and his tireless labors on behalf of Native American Catholics and the cause of canonization for Saint Kateri.

FOREWORD

by Monsignor Paul A. Lenz,
Executive Director Emeritus, Bureau of Catholic Indian Missions,
Washington, D.C., and vice-postulator for the Cause for
Canonization of Kateri Tekakwitha

When the beatification of Blessed Kateri Tekakwitha took place at Saint Peter's Basilica in the Vatican on June 20, 1980, as the national director of the Bureau of Catholic Indian Missions of the United States, I was assigned to be in charge of necessary details. A large pilgrimage for the beatification liturgy was organized and a group of several hundred went to Rome.

While in Rome a request came to me for an interview on worldwide Vatican Radio. One of the first questions I was asked was, "Did Kateri Tekakwitha really live, or has she just been a name to please the Indians?" I was grateful for the question because it gave me the opportunity to tell of the tremendous amount of written information prepared by the Jesuit missionaries before she died, and of the incredible number of books that have been written since her death in 1680 to the present day.

For the canonization of Blessed Kateri, one miracle was needed by the Congregation for the Causes of Saints at the Vatican. I was named by the Vatican as the vice-postulator to assist Father Paul Molinari, S.J., the postulator in Rome. With a dedicated tribunal from the Archdiocese of Seattle, it took almost three years of work and investigation, but the miracle of a six-year-old Indian boy, Jacob "Jake" Finkbonner, being totally cured from a flesh-eating disease, necrotizing fasciitis, was approved. When doctors could not find that any of their expertise or medicines were the cause of the cure, it became certain that the thousands of prayers and the laying on of a relic of Blessed Kateri to Jacob's body were the reasons she interceded for the cure.

This book, *Saint Kateri: Lily of the Mohawks,* gives account after account about the saintly life Kateri lived and highlights how the Jesuit priests were aware of the wonderful, truly devout Mohawk Indian. Father Jacques de Lamberville, S.J., was the first priest to recognize the spiritual qualities in the youthful Kateri. Jesuit Fathers Claude Chauchetière and Pierre Cholenec also spent much time praying with her and writing many pages while observing her holiness. Detailing what the Jesuits wrote of her before she died and compiling much about the appearances of Kateri and the miracles worked by her after her death, this book offers readers an intimate look at the life and spiritual legacy of the saintly Kateri Tekakwitha.

TIMELINE

c. 1000 The ancestors of the Iroquois settle in the Finger Lakes region in New York.

1492 Christopher Columbus reaches the New World. At the time of his arrival, it is estimated that there were twenty million Native Americans spread out across North and South America; approximately two million inhabited North America.

1534 to 1541 The French Jacques Cartier explores parts of North America; his accounts capture the imagination of France.

c. 1550 The Iroquois League, or Five Nations, is established among the Mohawk, Onondaga, Oneida, Cayuga, and Seneca under the leadership of Dekanawidah, the Great Peacemaker, and Hiawatha. By the early seventeenth century, the Iroquois reach their zenith of power in North America, with a population of approximately twelve thousand.

1604 The French establish the earliest temporary French mission in what became the United States, probably on an island in Passamaquoddy Bay, between Maine and New Brunswick.

c. 1608 Samuel de Champlain visits the area of the Saint Lawrence River Valley and encounters native peoples. He founds the great city of Québec, which becomes the capital of New France.

1609 The Iroquois League begins the Beaver Wars with the French and their allies, the Huron, over control of the fur trade in the Northeast.

1615 The Dutch start a trading post at Orange, modern-day Albany, New York. That same year, the first French missionaries, four Recollect Franciscans, arrive.

1625 The first Jesuits arrive in Canada, and the "Black Robes," as they were called, set out to evangelize the wilderness of North America.

1628 The Mohawk defeat the Mohican Indians and secure control of the fur trade with the Dutch.

1642 The great Jesuit Saint Isaac Jogues is captured with several companions, including fellow missionary Saint René Goupil, by the Mohawk. Goupil is martyred, and Jogues endures unspeakable tortures that leave him terribly mutilated.

1645 A peace treaty is signed between the Iroquois and the Huron, Algonquin, and French.

1646 French Jesuit missionaries set out to evangelize among the Mohawk. Fathers Jogues and Jean de Lalande are martyred by the Mohawk in the village of Ossernenon (modern Auriesville and Albany, New York) on October 18, 1646. Others follow in death, including the Jesuit priests Anthony Daniel, Jean de Brébeuf, Gabriel Lalemant, Charles Garnier, and Noel Chabanel. With Goupil and Jogues, the martyrs were canonized in 1930 by Pope Pius XI and are honored as the North American Martyrs.

1648–1650 The Iroquois wage a war on the Huron, allies of the French, during which thousands of the Huron are slaughtered. The remnant of the Huron relocate near Québec City and finally settle at Wendake.

1654 The French establish a trading and missionary center at Onondaga (in present-day New York). It is attacked the next year by the Mohawk after a smallpox epidemic.

1656 Saint Kateri Tekakwitha is born at Ossernenon, at the Mohawk fortress called Gandaouague.

1660 Tekakwitha's village suffers from a severe outbreak of smallpox, and the epidemic claims her parents. She is taken into the care of her uncle. The village is moved to Auries Creek, where they establish the new village of Gandawague.

1665 Three of the Five Nations of the Iroquois League make peace with the French; the Mohawk and Oneida refuse to join in the treaty.

1666–1667 The governor of New France sends the Carignan Regiment under the Marquis de Tracy to make war on the Mohawk and the Oneida.

1668 The two tribes make peace with the French and permit missionaries to enter their lands and villages. Father Jean Pierron, S.J., is stationed in the Mohawk village of Tekakwitha's clan. He is replaced in 1670 by Father Francis Boniface, S.J.

1674 Father Boniface dies suddenly and is succeeded by Father Jacques de Lamberville, S.J.

1676 On April 5, Tekakwitha is baptized and given the name Kateri, after Saint Catherine of Siena.

1677 The Iroquois establish an alliance with the English, through what is called the Covenant Chain. Kateri leaves her village and settles in the mission of Saint Francis Xavier of Sault Saint-Louis, a haven for Native American Catholics near Montréal. On the morning of Christmas Day, Kateri makes her first holy Communion.

1679 On March 25, Kateri makes a vow of perpetual virginity.

1680 On April 17, Kateri dies at the age of twenty-four.

1684 The Jesuits decide to move Kateri's remains from the mission cemetery to the church at the Sault Mission.

1687 Jacques-René de Brisay de Denonville, Marquis de Denonville, governor of New France, wages war on the Iroquois. He is defeated in 1689.

1719 After moving the mission several times and bringing Kateri's remains with them, the Catholics of the Sault Mission bring her relics to rest at the mission at Kahnawake (modern-day Caughnawaga, Canada) in a case made of ebony. At the same time, some of her relics are distributed to other Native American mission outposts.

1721 The Iroquois renew the Covenant Chain through the Treaty at Albany. In the next years, the English continue to encroach on the territory of the Native Americans.

1744 The Iroquois sell their claim to the Shenandoah Valley to Virginia for two hundred pounds in gold through the Treaty of Lancaster.

1754–1763 The French and Indian War (the North American name for Europe's Seven Years' War) ends with the defeat of

France. The 1763 Treaty of Paris calls for France to cede Canada to England. It signals the demise of New France.

1763 The Jesuits are expelled from New France.

1773 The Society of Jesus is suppressed by Pope Clement XIV, and the British confiscate all Jesuit property in Canada.

1775–1783 The American Revolution occurs, ending with the independence of the British colonies from England. The Iroquois League is divided in its sympathies. In the decades after the war, the Iroquois are driven from their lands in New York.

1800 The last Jesuit priest in Canada dies in Quebec.

1814 Pope Pius VII reconstitutes the Society of Jesus.

1842 The Jesuits are finally allowed to return to Canada, and on July 23, 1843, they celebrate the restoration of the cross over Kateri's original burial place.

1884 During the Third Plenary Council of Baltimore, the Jesuit Fathers ask the bishops of the United States to give their support to a petition to be sent to Pope Leo XIII, asking that causes for canonization be introduced for the Jesuit martyrs René Goupil and Isaac Jogues, and for Kateri Tekakwitha.

1930 The North American Martyrs are canonized by Pope Pius XI.

1931 The Diocese of Albany officially begins its own process of investigation into the life and possible heroic virtue of Kateri.

1932 The petition for the start of the cause is sent to Rome and is given its official start on July 11, 1932.

1938 The *positio* for the cause is submitted to authorities in the Congregation for the Causes of Saints with the intention of demonstrating the heroic virtue of Kateri.

1943 The *positio* is accepted by the congregation, and on January 3, 1943, Pope Pius XII declares Kateri venerable.

1980 Kateri is beatified in Rome on June 22, 1980, by Pope Blessed John Paul II, with several other blessed, or *beati*.

2011 On December 19, Pope Benedict XVI accepts the recommendation of the congregation and formally approves a miracle achieved through the intercession of Kateri, thereby paving the way for her canonization.

2012 Kateri Tekakwitha is canonized at the Vatican on October 21, 2012.

INTRODUCTION

Saint Kateri Tekakwitha was seemingly far from remarkable. A member of the Native American tribe of the Mohawk in the American northeastern territories, she lived long before the British colonists decided to sever their ties with their homeland and forge a new nation in the wilderness. Her biographical facts state that she was born in 1656 and died in 1680. She converted to the Catholic faith in 1676, faced persecution by her own people, and had to find sanctuary in the Mission of Saint Francis Xavier of Sault Saint-Louis near modern Montréal. There she lived for two years before her death on April 17, 1680.

As word spread across eastern New York and then across the vast territory of New France of the woman's death, it was greeted with mourning among the Native Americans and the French colonists equally. But what was remarkable was that as the sad announcement was taken from village to village and settlement to settlement, in many places there was no need to say her name. A letter would arrive or a traveler would bring the news. All that was needed was a simple sentence:

"The saint is dead."

For those who understood who was meant, there was no need for further explanation. Many had already heard the stories and accounts of her life, and in the months and years after her death, there was the added testimony of men and women whose lives had been changed through her intercession.

The "Saint," as she was called, was not some powerful leader in New France; nor was she a prominent woman religious superior; nor was she even a chieftain among the Native American peoples who still dominated whole parts of North America. She was a twenty-four-year-old Indian maiden who could barely walk into the sunshine because of the lingering effects of smallpox and whose face had been disfigured by the terrible disease that had taken most of her family. She could claim no worldly achievements, had few possessions, and led a brief and apparently insignificant life. Indeed, she lived on earth as a Catholic for only four years.

And yet she was revered, both in the time before and in the time after her death.

The October 21, 2012, canonization of Saint Kateri by Pope Benedict XVI was the culmination of a modern process of canonization that officially began in 1932, when the Holy See gave formal recognition to the Diocese of Albany's request for the cause for canonization to be started. It advanced slowly until 1980, when she was beatified by Pope Blessed John Paul II, and it was brought to its joyous conclusion with her being raised to the altars and proclaimed a saint in Rome in 2012.

The process by which the Church proclaims a woman or a man a saint is an arduous one, and it can take many years to reach a final determination. In Saint Kateri's case, centuries passed before her cause was opened, but as is documented in Chapter Ten, there were definite historical circumstances that caused the long delay. Indeed, she was beloved as a holy person before her death and revered as a beloved figure afterward. But a cause for canonization requires more than merely a reputation for holiness. The Church properly asks for clear evidence that the person in question left a powerful spiritual legacy that moved and encouraged others to embrace the faith with the same fervor and love of Christ. The Church also asks for proof that the candidate led a life that exemplified not merely trying to live the virtues, but that the virtues were perfected to a heroic degree. Finally, there is the requirement of certified miracles that took place through the candidate's intercession. Saint Kateri Tekakwitha fulfilled every one of these requirements.

The brief but exceptional life of the saint was documented in surprising detail by the Jesuit missionaries who first met her, taught her the truths of the Catholic faith, baptized her, heard her confessions, gave her the sacraments, and finally helped her enter into life eternal. Our knowledge of Saint Kateri would be all but nonexistent had it not been for the letters, accounts, and biographies penned by the Black Robes, as the Jesuits were called, who served with such fidelity at the Sault Mission. Three in particular proved able witnesses to Saint Kateri's conversion, development, and love of the sacraments and the Church: Fathers Jacques de Lamberville, Pierre Cholenec, and Claude Chauchetière.

To be sure, the priests wrote with the cultural biases of the age — for example, they regularly used the term "savages" ("sauvages") to describe the Native Americans. While holding a somewhat condescending view of the Indians, the priests nevertheless had a true and abiding concern for the material, and especially for the spiritual, welfare of the Native Americans in general and for the converted Indians in particular.

The biographies of Saint Kateri that were penned at the time, especially by Fathers Cholenec and Chauchetière, convey deeply moving experiences, but they are also clearly intended to argue for her perfection of the virtues to a heroic degree and for the spiritual legacy she bequeathed not only to her own people but to people across the whole of New France. Both priests focused heavily, for example, on enumerating and detailing the specific virtues Saint Kateri had perfected. The methodical Jesuits essentially built a case for her sanctity and were careful to include eyewitness testimony from those who benefited from her holiness in the time she was alive and after she had died. Their accounts are valuable to any historian or biographer, but they are also excellent samples of hagiographical writings in the great tradition of the Church. They are, in effect, the building blocks for the *positio*, or formal case for her heroic virtue and holiness, that was sent to Rome some three centuries after her death.

What makes their testimony even more pertinent is precisely the presence of their cultural biases. Far from downplaying Saint Kateri's fervent desire for holiness or dismissing it as the excessive eagerness of a supposed "savage" imitating those who had taught her, the priests wrote in awe of her spiritual development and her perfection of the virtues to a heroic degree. They were humbled by her sanctity, and they wanted the rest of New France, the Jesuit Order, and the whole Church to know about it. Their work had its effect, certainly. She was known across Eastern Canada and then in Europe, with stories about her reaching even the royal court of France. The fall of New France to the armies of England in 1759 prevented the cause of Kateri — and other heroic figures who built the Catholic Church in Canada — from being developed fully. The restoration of the ecclesiastical life in Canada in the nineteenth century helped bring to light the powerful legacy of Saint Kateri, which had not died, but had been cast into shadow by the events of the intervening centuries.

The question can be asked about Kateri's relevance for the modern world and for today's Catholics. Saint Kateri is a sign of the faith in the New World. The Black Robes and other missionaries arrived in North America and set out for the wilderness to proclaim the Gospel. Many — such as Saint Isaac Jogues and the other North American Martyrs — were slain in Indian villages and in the forests, but their deaths were not in vain. Native Americans responded to their preaching, and the blood of these martyrs helped plant the Catholic Church in what became the United States. Kateri Tekakwitha was one of those who responded to Christ's call, and in so doing she became the first Native American to be canonized a saint, joining Saint Juan Diego and Saint Rose of Lima in the ranks of the first indigenous saints of the Americas.

Saint Kateri is also a beautiful example of an important truth that Pope Blessed John Paul II stressed throughout his pontificate: She shows us all that saints are found in every country and in every walk of life and situation. Holiness is not limited to monks and nuns and priests and popes. Nor is it limited to certain demographic groups or to those of European backgrounds. It is attainable by everyone, regardless of where they live or of their specific cultural circumstances. For women and men all over the world, Saint Kateri pointed the way to the universality of holiness and so to Christ. She tells us that where the faith is inculturated, where Christ is offered in ways that are comprehensible to native peoples, he will be given welcome. Equally, Saint Kateri demonstrates that it is possible to be a faithful and holy Catholic while still embodying the very best of her culture. The two are not mutually exclusive; being Catholic does not mean rejecting the love of one's people, group, or country. Archbishop Charles Chaput, O.F.M. Cap. — the archbishop of Philadelphia, a member of the Prairie Band Potawatomi tribe, and the only Native American Catholic archbishop in the United States — said of Saint Kateri in an interview with Catholic News Service: "We are all very proud of her because she embodies in herself what Pope Blessed John Paul II called inculturation — the saints are the truly inculturated members of a particular ethnic group because they personally embody both the Gospel and the culture from which they come."

In this sense, Saint Kateri is also honored today as a patron of ecology, along with Saint Francis of Assisi. Like the rest of her people, she understood the importance of finding balance with the natural world and of exercising a proper stewardship of the earth's resources. These are consonant with Catholic teaching, as Pope Benedict XVI has expressed with great vigor throughout his time as pontiff.

She was likewise a powerful role model for prayer. The priests who wrote about her life went into great detail about her commitment to prayer and contemplation of God and the Eucharist. She spent every spare moment in prayer in the mission chapel, and while at work in the village she sanctified these menial tasks with prayer, offering them up to Christ. She conformed her sufferings to the Cross, offered her life to Christ, and proclaimed his name even up to her very last breath. For her gifts of contemplative prayer, she has been called the "Mystic in the Wilderness."

Finally, Saint Kateri is a role model for Native Americans, and in particular for Native American Catholics who love the Catholic faith even as they labor to preserve their own traditions, language, and heritage.

Few racial or ethnic groups have suffered the peculiar travesties of justice endured by the various tribes of Native American people in the United States, a condition that remains unabated in some regions even today. Since the time of the first European intrusion into the Americas, the native populations have been plagued by misconceptions about their origins, their societies, their philosophies, and even their spiritual ideals. Such misunderstandings, based on brief encounters, legends, or tall tales, and nurtured by indifference or prejudice, have robbed many tribal communities of their lustrous heritage and have reduced their singular accomplishments in the eyes of their fellow citizens.

Native American Catholics have endured many different forms of persecution. As members of the Native American peoples, they faced bigotry, intolerance, and cruel indifference as whites wrested away control of the continent and fulfilled the demands of Manifest Destiny, the self-appointed drive to bring all of North America into the United States. There followed relentless wars and diseases that eroded their numbers; eviction from their lands and placement on reservations; the

Code of Indian Offences of 1883, which prohibited traditional Indian customs; the Dawes Allotment Act of 1887, which divided up the reservations for individual ownership and which both obliterated tribal life and left Indian lands subject to unscrupulous acquisition by white settlers; and the culmination, the Wounded Knee Massacre on December 29, 1890. Native American Catholics faced even more prejudice from the government, and from their own people. To hold to the Catholic faith under such circumstances is a great testament to the faith and the fortitude of Native American Catholics, and Saint Kateri has long been a model for both. As a patron saint of Native Americans, she can truly be honored as the "Glory of Many Nations."

As we consider the legacy of Saint Kateri among Native Americans, we note that the 2003 report by the United States Conference of Catholic Bishops, "Native American Catholics at the Millennium," records that nearly three million people identify themselves as Native American. Of these, 580,000, or 20 percent of the total population, belonging to more than three hundred tribes and nations in the United States and Canada, are considered Catholic. Native Americans comprise 3.5 percent of all Catholics in the United States. More than three hundred forty parishes in the United States serve predominantly Native American congregations, and 30 percent of all dioceses and archdioceses have an office that serves Native American Catholics. For all Native Americans, though, Kateri's canonization has special meaning.

This biography is the final edition of a book first published by Our Sunday Visitor in 1992, when Saint Kateri was still

Blessed Kateri and prayers for her canonization were ongoing. It is intended to serve as a basic introduction to the life and holiness of Kateri Tekakwitha, and to mark the joy surrounding her canonization. It is for those who are just now becoming familiar with her as a result of her being declared a saint, as well as for those who have long loved her and seen in her a great example for holiness. She is the "Lily of the Mohawks." This is her story.

PART ONE

THE WORLDS OF SAINT KATERI

Loving Creator God, we acknowledge your power and presence in the Four Directions of your vast and beautiful universe. We celebrate Kateri Tekakwitha, "Lily of the Mohawks," as one of your Son's most faithful followers.

Prayer from the National Kateri Tekakwitha Shrine in Fonda (Caughnawaga), New York

Chapter One

THE GREAT WILDERNESS

I traced in my heart the history of your tribes and nations.
I was able to see you as the noble descendants of countless
generations of inhabitants of this land, whose ways were marked
by great respect for the natural resources of land and rivers, of
forest and plain and desert. . . .

Pope Blessed John Paul II to Native Americans, 1987

It was long commonplace to refer to the Native American people as Indians, so much so that even they have referred to themselves as such because of the decades of general use of the term. Native Americans received the name Indians early on as a result of the misunderstanding of where the first Europeans to reach the New World had actually arrived. Native Americans have nothing to do with the Indian people of the Asian subcontinent. The name came to be used by Europeans after Christopher Columbus reached the New World in 1492. Columbus was not seeking a new exotic continent, however, but a passage to the East, known then for its spices, silks, jewels, and luxury goods. Because of the tales of Marco Polo and other determined adventurers who had managed to make the long journey across the Silk Road, the East had become an almost mythical place. Columbus believed that he had reached the "Indies," or East India, as that part of the world was called in Europe at the time. The name he thus coined for the American territories and for its inhabitants not only became popular, but part of the European vocabulary.

Until that fateful day more than five hundred years ago, few in Europe had ever contemplated the remote possibility of an entire continent rising out of the ocean between the Old World and the fabled "Indies." Certainly no major European power had ever mounted costly expeditions to America before Columbus stumbled upon it. The fact that he and his co-adventurers discovered the New World while busily seeking another place entirely did not alter the outcome of the event.

Native Americans, the Indians of the New World, have also been called "redskins" by their fellow countrymen over the centuries. The *positio* of the "Historical Section of the Sacred Congregation of Rites on the Introduction of the Cause for Beatification and Canonization and on the Virtues of the Servant of God, Katherine Tekakwitha, the Lily of the Mohawks," with an introduction dated 1938, states: "The servant of God Katherine Tekakwitha was a North American Indian, a genuine redskin, the first of that great and sorely tried human family to be presented to the Sacred Congregation of Rites as a candidate for the honors of the altar."

The term "redskin" is so engrained in the American consciousness, in fact, that it has become a part of Western lore. The word appears to have come from the French *peaux rouges,* or "red skins." Early French trappers and hunters, who scoured the Canadian and American wilds for furs, encountered the Native Americans, or Indians, and described them to their companions as *peaux rouges,* providing the basis for the tradition.

"Redskins" served the purpose of describing Native Americans to advancing white settlers, and it endured. Films, books, television shows, and even professional sports teams made the word part of the American cultural lexicon, although in recent decades it has been recognized as a pejorative, and its use in modern language has been discouraged.

Meanwhile, however, the Europeans of the Old World were beginning to hear of the discovery of such people in the wilderness of America. As tales of their lifestyles, their wars, and their arts trickled back to Europe, speculation about their origins became the rage. There was even a suggestion that Native Americans were actually part of the lost tribes of Israel. This idea opened up fervent debates and controversies in Europe's academic and religious circles, but such arguments remained in Europe. The settlers and hunters in the New World started to push their way into the untamed continent and had little time to debate possible biblical connections when they met up with local tribes.

The Europeans who had come to America as settlers and hunters were quite single-minded. Some came to claim as many fur-bearing animals as possible during each hunting season. Some came to stake out new homesteads and seize the wilderness as their own. The mountain men, the hunters and explorers who ranged far and wide over plains and mountains — the first uniquely American byproducts of the wilderness — gained intimate knowledge of the various native communities, for good or for ill. They either became good friends or feared enemies of the tribes. Individualists who looked down on anyone who needed the trappings of civilization in order to survive, mountain men disliked the settlers and the colonists even more than they did the Indians.

The settlers chiefly wanted the land that belonged to the tribes, just as the Europeans, and later the United States government and the states, desired it for economic development, for agriculture, and as places for the growing white population to live. Many volumes have been written about the process of settling the New World and the ways in which the Indians, despite their original generosity and kindnesses, were rolled back by the relentless tides of immigrants and land grabbers.

Today, the term "Native American" has taken root. It not only demonstrates the fact that everyone else calling himself or herself an American and claiming the United States home is a newcomer to its shores or a descendant of one, but the term also clearly depicts the centuries of residence in America of the various tribal groupings, which can be verified scientifically.

The original ancestors of the Indians were of Mongolian or some other Asiatic stock. It is known that these ancestors came into the American continent from Siberia between twelve thousand and thirty-five thousand years ago, perhaps even earlier. They began their endless treks when *homo sapiens* were expanding their social skills in the face of a restless and hostile world.

Life in the Siberian tundra, where most ancestors of the Native Americans originated, was harsh and demanding even in good times. The freezing temperatures, the winds roaring over the marshy plains, the storms that raged over glacier peaks, and the wild animals that roamed the regions threatened their progress as they moved ever eastward into the unknown lands of a new continent. Nomadic or semi-nomadic in their lifestyles, these groups were linked to the seasonal changes of the earth and to the migrations of the game animals they hunted for sustenance.

These human beings were living in the last stages of the Great Ice Age. In the fourth and final movements of the polar ice formations, called the Wisconsin Glaciation (in Europe designated the Wurm Glaciation), the entire Northern Hemisphere of the earth was locked in the embrace of giant glaciers. These vast mounds of ice and snow, as deep as fifty feet in some areas, inched steadily southward, leveling small peaks and ripping apart forests and glades. Most of the land features known today were invisible as the original formations were erased by the glaciers moving inch by inch toward the American Great Lakes. Everything in the path of such massive mountains of snow and ice was molded into a barren wasteland, frozen and gutted by the cold and by the pressures of the weight. In turn, the sea levels at the time were probably from two hundred to four hundred feet lower than they are today.

Between Alaska of the New World and Siberia of the Old, now separated by the Bering Straits, there was a land mass, believed by some to have been approximately a thousand miles wide. This land mass, now called Beringia, served as a bridge between Asia and North America — rising and falling, settling and thickening as the glaciers edged their way forward on their southern journeys or suffered changes in the warming winds. Beringia was probably not much more than a water-soaked plain most of the time, a favorite haunt for migrating herds and smaller types of game, including those animals that preyed on the great masses of other animals moving across the horizon. These herds were the lure for the ancestors of the Indians, bringing them onto the frozen meadows and marshes of Beringia to seek their food. As the herds wandered farther afield, entering the American continent, the hunting tribes followed. Behind them their clans and their families straggled along, entering the New World that beckoned through the mists and the snows.

These human beings certainly did not set out to claim a new continent for their own kind. They had no idea that they were about to settle a New World. These were primitive people, carrying simple weapons, hunting and gathering in the wake of the migrating herds, and stopping only to build campfires and to rest when the herds appeared to have settled or when their meager stocks were sufficient to support them for a time. They wore pelts and skins, and they ate what they could find, using basic tools and utensils.

Beringia would have looked like just another stretch of land opening before them as they moved ever onward in search of meat and skins. The idea of a continental bridge was far beyond them, and would not have been within the scope of their reasoning. In time, of course, that bridge collapsed, washed away with the great chunks of ice that were entering the sea as the glaciers withdrew and gave birth to the Bering Sea. With their only avenue of retreat closed behind them, if they even thought of such a retreat, the groups were forced to remain on the American continent. It is probable that these tribes made no attempt to retrace their steps at all, as one territory in that climate looked like another. The earth, however, was giving way to warming trends, and the ice and the freezing temperatures were becoming seasonal. As the clans trekked southward, seeking sheltering caves and passageways through the remaining ice fields, they followed the herds seeking their own fresh domains.

It is believed that these first Native Americans followed the modern Brooks Range through the Mackenzie River Valley or wandered south through the Yukon. Their far-ranging journeys are astounding, considering the fact that some crossed the territory encompassing the entire United States, with many going as far as South America and the Andes in time. The great cultures that arose in the regions of Mesoamerica and present-day Peru are testaments to the vulnerable human beings who made these treks in primitive conditions, and on foot.

Sites from the historical Paleo-Indian Period, which is divided into Early and Late and covers the period from 15,000 BC to 8,000 BC, have been uncovered all across North America. These range from Onion Portage, Alaska, to Tepexpan, Mexico — where remains of mammoth hunters have been discovered — and from Laguna Beach, California, to the Plenge Site in Warren County, New Jersey. Such sites demonstrate the great flexibility of these first migrants, who staked out their own lands and then adapted to the demands of the local environments.

Distinct ages of evolutional development can be documented in the remains found in these places, determined by the presence of stone weapon points, such as Clovis, Folsom, and Plano. Each new era represented changes and improved skills as the people discovered new methods of insuring their survival and new ways of pooling their resources for the benefit of all.

The migrants moved steadily across North America as others trekked southward. Each region, now called microenvironments, offered them a variety of fruits, nuts, small animals, fish, birds, herbs, and grasses. They learned to band together to hunt larger game, or megafauna, as they became skilled at fortifying their settlements against attacks by wild animals. There was a great diversity of large game in this period. The three-ton woolly mammoth roamed the plains alongside the American mastadon, the giant sloth, the American lion, and camelids, whose surviving descendants still exist in South America in the form of llamas, guanacos, and vicunas. The dire wolves, believed by some scholars to have stood six feet at the shoulders, bears, tapirs, saber-toothed tigers, the great bison, and giant beavers — some weighing as much as three hundred pounds — roamed the hills and plains along with smaller peccaries, small piglike mammals.

As the tribes extended their hunting ranges and began experiments with lifestyles that were adapted to the seasons and to their new environments, changes took place within their ranks. Some groups perished because they could not manage the harsh threats that loomed before them at every turn of the trail. Others were incorporated into larger, more self-sufficient groups that emerged in sizable homelands. New weapons were developed, new ways of defending themselves against animals or of stalking them as prey, and a social order grew up as their skills increased.

The Native Americans were at home in the New World, where they would craft their spiritual and religious concepts — especially those of a cosmogonic nature, which explained the universe and the role of human beings. These Indians asked themselves the primordial questions that have haunted humanity since the beginning of time: They asked about their origins, about their short time upon the earth, and about their ultimate destiny beyond the grave. At the same time, they became one with nature and with the seasons, forming their unique sense of the earth, of the land, and of the sky and the elements. With this relationship came a definite sense of stewardship, of care and concern for all living things.

CHAPTER TWO

THE NATIVE AMERICANS

The early encounter between your traditional cultures and the European way of life was an event of such significance and change that it profoundly influences your collective life even today. That encounter was a harsh and painful reality for your peoples.

Pope Blessed John Paul II to Native Americans, 1987

By the time Columbus reached the New World in 1492, it is estimated that there were twenty million Native Americans spread out across North and South America. There were approximately two million inhabitants of North America, a rich tapestry of tribes with established cultures.

The American wilderness was the most basic landscape in Kateri Tekakwitha's existence, a force that not only shaped the native groups residing there but altered the outlook of the Europeans who crowded on its shores. At the close of the Archaic Period, around 300 B.C., the American continent was home to many tribal communities, each one developing the specific characteristics that would mark their presence in the forests and plains. Their various geographical locations enforced the differing lifestyles on the tribes, and warfare among them led them into expansions or migrations to even more distant wild lands.

In the Southwest, for example, the ruins of the Anasazi clearly demonstrate that they recognized the need for strategic defenses. The Adena Mounds, the Hopewell Culture, and others in the Midwest depict a well-established death cult, as well as a confederated government. Monks Mound in Missouri, for instance, was one hundred feet high, almost as tall as the Great Pyramid of Giza in Egypt. The site is believed to have been the abode of as many as thirty thousand to forty thousand Native Americans.

The desert nomadic tribes followed their flocks into other areas, and farms emerged in the Southwest, linked by trade with the towering civilizations of Mesoamerica, such as the Aztecs and Maya. These trade routes, expanding farms, mounds, and trapping sites in the forests blended into the first homelands.

In the northeastern part of America, where Kateri would live, forests and woodlands covered most of the region at the close of the Archaic Period. Oaks, hickories, chestnuts, and other trees formed expanses of thick foliage, interspersed by glades, rivers, lakes, and plains. Within these woods a rich variety of plants and animals flourished, drawing early tribal communities to the rich resources and natural havens.

Many indications of early habitation have been documented in this part of the United States, including ceramics and signs of an evolving burial-ritual system that used cremation. Such a burial system indicates a growing religious sense — the asking of the primordial questions — and the awareness of the spiritual side of human existence. The Forest People of North America, as the early inhabitants of the northeastern United States are now called, used all the natural resources at hand in their chosen lands. The trees of the forest, the bark especially, for example, provided the raw material for the walls of their residences, and were used as well for spears, arrows, trays, canoes, stakes, litters, nets, and snowshoes. Within the forests there were nuts, fruits, wild fowls, rabbits, woodchucks, beaver, moose, elk, caribou, deer, antelope, sheep, and bears, which assumed, along with the eagle, positions of ceremonial power and deep religious significance.

The Forest People lived in wigwams, which were erected by taking four saplings and bending them toward the center as a framework. Tree bark was then stretched and fastened into place as walls. The interior floors of the wigwams were covered with swamp grass and fir branches. This was then covered with moose hides and used as sleeping pallets. Other pelts were used as rugs, or as bits of ornamentation, including those of the North American wolf, coyote, fox, wolverine, rabbit, raccoon, weasel, skunk, gopher, marmot, squirrel, chipmunk, marten, beaver, ermine, mink, and even mice.

The wigwam differed from the teepee, or *tipi*, depicted in historical photographs and paintings of the Plains People. The teepee was made with three or four main poles, supported by twenty to twenty-four lesser poles, and standing as high as twenty feet and measuring thirty feet across. The teepee was

43

collapsible and could be moved when the migrations with the herds began.

The Forest People, Kateri's clans, were not a nomadic people, but used hunters, called the Woodland Warriors, to keep the larders stocked. These hunters were solitary, patient, and famously strong. They had a particular sensitivity to the landscapes of their regions, and they understood even the most subtle changes in sound and movement about them, which made them renowned hunters. Birds and animals manifested alarm when strangers were in the vicinity, and also, along with plants, underwent changes signaling the coming of a new season. The spring melt was evident, as was the coming of the hot, dry winds of summers. By becoming one with the animals and plants of the forests, the Woodland Warriors used every sense to track and locate game, to protect themselves from peril, and to scout for enemy raiding parties that could endanger their villages. Some women in the tribes proved themselves skilled in these capacities and were so honored. Alongside the men they preserved the land and its resources, and demonstrated a sense of oneness with the woodlands that served them so faithfully.

By A.D. 500, the bow and the arrow had been invented and was used alongside spears and lances with flint tips. Each tribe had from five to ten principal hunters. The bows used by these Woodland Warriors were made from the ash, yew, or mulberry tree, bent into shape over hot ashes. Some had bone inlays or sinew, and twisted fibers strengthened the ends or the middle of the bow.

Arrows were designed in individual styles, easily recognized by other tribes, and later by the settlers. The feathers of eagles, buzzards, turkeys, or hawks normally decorated them. Great hunters could shoot targets fifty yards away, and they could pull arrows from their quivers quickly for rapid-fire volleys, shooting on and on against enemies. Some tribes, including the Iroquois, are reported to have used eight-foot blowguns that shot poisoned darts feathered with thistledown.

The Forest People carried fire from one camp to another when moving on to seasonal sites. Such moves were normally dependent on changing weather conditions and the signs of coming freezes, as the tribes sought shelter for the harsh winter months. Fields were cultivated in certain seasons of the year; flint corn, for example, was planted in May and harvested in June. Squash, beans, pumpkins, gourds, sweet potatoes, manioc, tomatoes, nuts, and a form of tobacco (*Nicotiana rustica*) were also either cultivated or regularly gathered.

Most of the Woodland People wore skins, cleaned and prepared, fashioned into leggings and shirts or blouses and skirts. Loincloths were made out of deerskin, and mantles, or capes, were used in colder months. These articles of clothing were decorated with quills, eagle feathers, shells, and beads; jewelry was popular, especially items made out of stone and copper.

~ ~ ~

The world of the Iroquois, one of the major Forest People groups, forms the second landscape of Kateri's life on earth. It was formulated by the first landscape, the rugged American wilderness, but it was a highly complex environment that took into consideration the needs of the weak and the infirm as well as those who could make constant contributions to the well-being of the tribe.

The Iroquois were called by that name by the French because they supposedly ended most of their sentences with the word *hiro*, which means "I have spoken," and *koue*, the sound of a small cry, probably made for emphasis. The tribe called itself the *Ho-dé-no-sau-nee,* "the people of the longhouses." Historians have honored the Iroquois with the title the "Romans of the New World" because of their governmental system and their intelligent, reasoned concept of citizen participation on all levels. The enemies of the Iroquois called them the "Kinsmen of the Wolves." This was an honorable title, one given with respect, in deference to the relentless ferocity of the Iroquois when attacked. The Iroquois spoke their own language, which was related to the Algonquin and the Macro-Siouan tongues.

By the time the first European settlers entered the American wilderness and the domain of the Iroquois, which was quite vast, the various groups that constituted the Iroquois were settled in their homelands, which they guarded fiercely. The Iroquois were comfortable in their deciduous birch, beech, maple, and elm forests, which gave way to firs and spruce in the higher elevations. The Iroquois territory consisted of the land south of Lake Ontario, roughly modern New York State, a region dotted by streams, valleys, and hills. The Finger Lakes were in their domain, and there the Mohawk River flowed into the Appalachian Mountains. In Eastern Iroquois, as the first Canadians named the area, there were stands of oak, chestnuts, and poplars, broken by the valleys of the Hudson River tributaries.

It is believed that the Iroquois migrated from the regions north of the Saint Lawrence River, although there are some references to them in the records of the Pawnees, which would place their origins far west of the Mississippi River. It is now accepted by many scholars that the original inhabitants of the region claimed in time by the Iroquois were the Owasco, a farming people who raised corn crops on many sites as early as AD 1300.

The Iroquois were also farmers, despite their fame as Woodland Warriors. They used the swidden, or slash-and-burn technique, for preparing land for crops and harvests. They cut down stands of trees in order to claim new fields, setting fire to the remaining trunks, the flames also devouring the low-lying shrubs in the same plots. The resulting ashes were used as fertilizer for the claimed land. Each new field prepared by this technique was then tilled until it became barren. It was then abandoned, and the farmers moved on to the next area. Relying chiefly on farming for sustenance could thus result in wholesale devastation of vast tracts of land.

The Iroquois were perhaps saved from land decimation by the fact that they relied more on hunting and gathering than on cultivation of crops. Consequently, the land's resources were not as quickly taxed. It has been estimated that each community used as many as two thousand deer each season. The animal was eaten, and clothing, weapons, and utensils were manufactured out of its carcass. The crops that were grown by the Iroquois included three that they revered as bountiful nurturers of life. They called them the "Three Sisters," and they were usually corn, squash, and beans. Such crops could be stored for the lean months of winter, and they were lush and beautiful in the fields. Tobacco was another prized crop, grown for ceremonial uses, as the idea of smoke rising into the heavens was viewed as a salute to the Great Spirit and his heavenly companions.

The Iroquois people formed a confederation of several tribes around the fourteenth century AD, forming the second landscape in Kateri's life. The Five Nations Confederacy, the *Ho-de-no-sau-nee*, was composed of the following tribes:

- Mohawk — the *Ga-ne-a-ga-o-no* — the Flint-Possessing People;
- Oneida — the *Ona-yota-ka-o-no* — the People of the Stone;
- Onondaga — the *O-nun-da-ga-o-no* — the People on the Hills;
- Cayuga — the *Gue-u-gweh-o-no* — the People at the Mucky Lands (marshes);
- Seneca — the *Nun-da-wa-o-no* — the Great Hill People.

In time, the Tuscarora joined the federation as well, but in the beginning the lands held in common were divided into five strips, running north to south, ranging from the Hudson River to the shores of Lake Erie. Each tribe had its own lake or river system, and each region abounded in forests, hills, and natural resources. Such land divisions were called the "longhouse" (hence the name chosen by the tribes for the confederacy), and they averaged two hundred miles apart.

Within each longhouse the tribes maintained their own councils and their own ceremonial fires, symbols of authority, reason, and justice. The eastern door of the Five Nations, Iroquoia, was guarded by the Longhouse of the Mohawks, the people of Kateri Tekakwitha.

The Five Nations came into being because of a vision of a holy man named Dekanawidah (or Tekanawita), who in the middle of the sixteenth century dreamed of a region shared in common by former competitive tribes. This remarkable sage envisioned the Iroquois League joined under the Tree of Great Peace, *Kaianerekowa*, bonded in brotherhood, in mutual respect, and in the desire to protect the integrity and rights of each individual man and woman within its borders. Dekanawidah confided his dream to a Mohawk warrior named Hiawatha, and together they prepared a message for all the other tribes in the area.

Hiawatha then began to visit the villages of the tribes, speaking to the chiefs and the people before their campfires. He related how Dekanawidah had been given this great vision, which was a gift to the people from the Great Spirit. Oratory was one of the exquisite talents of the Iroquois, and with the image of the sacred tree, peace, and the tribes living as one against all enemies, came resolve. The elders and the tribal councils agreed to unite the people for the common good of all.

It was decided that each tribe would remain its own entity, nurturing the traditions and ideals that had been forged over the centuries in the American wilderness. Each of these groups had their own views of the earth and the roles of men and women, but they shared in common the concept of the "hearth" family, which consisted of a man and his wife and their offspring. These were related, in turn, to the members of the same matriarchal lineage — the family traced through the mother's ancestors — and then to the clan. The clans of the various nations had specific designations and duties. These included the Clans of the Turtle, Painted Turtle, the Great Name Bearers, the Ancient Name Bearers, the Great Bear, the Ancient Bear, the Large Snipe (or Plover), the Small Snipe (or Plover), the Hawk, the Deer, the Standing Rock, and so on. Several clans formed a tribe, that in turn formed the nation.

The Seneca are reported to have been the last to consent to the union, but eventually they saw the advantages of being part of a unique social experiment in a wild and often hostile world. Not only would the natural resources be shared and protected, but each nation could count on a unified military force. It has been estimated that the total Iroquois population at the time of Kateri Tekakwitha's life was approximately twenty-five thousand. Such a population could put three thousand men into the field easily, and they were well-trained warriors, working in a highly developed military fashion against their enemies. Warfare in the region had taken a grim toll over the centuries, and the Iroquois were determined to protect their domain. When the Seneca consented to join the Five Nations Confederacy, it was said that the members clasped hands "so firmly that a falling tree could not sever them." So stable and profitable did the organization prove, in fact, that within half a century the Five Nations were the most powerful Native Americans on the North American continent.

A Great Council, composed of representatives of the united tribes elected by the matriarchs, met at Onondaga, under the Tree of Great Peace, the mighty symbol that was such an integral part of Dekanawidah's vision. An eagle perched high on that mighty tree, according to tradition, keeping watch over the council. This confederation of representatives was called the Council of the Fifty Sachems, although after the initial gathering only forty-nine were ever present. The place designated for Hiawatha remained empty for all time after his passing, in memory of his courageous journey to bring union to the people. The sachems were chosen with specific virtues in mind. For example, they had to be honest men, able to remain above petty village or clan politics. Their symbol of office was the antlers of the deer, and the people gathered to witness their acceptance of the offices during their ceremonies of installation. A Conferring of Rank festival followed, with the new sachem catering the entire affair.

The Great Council Fire burned whenever the sachems were in session, and the smoke of that fire was a symbol far and wide that men of reason and goodwill had met to speak words of wisdom and justice. Such meetings were prolonged and filled with elegant oratory, and each one was opened by prayers of thanksgiving for the earth and all its natural resources, bestowed upon mankind by the Great Creator, called the source and ruler of health and of life. In this manner the council served as an extension of the Iroquois families and clans, and the members provided solutions for many of the problems the tribes had to overcome over the generations.

This was not a general court, however, and it was not available to the average Indian. Not everyone could walk up and address the sachems freely. If a crisis arose, such as a quarrel over property or rights, an individual had to discuss the matter first with his own family members, then with the clan elders, and then with the chiefs of the entire nation. Smaller issues were normally settled within one of those circles, and there was no need to bring it before the assembled representatives. Wars, trade affairs, contacts with Europeans, or threats from outsiders were commonly part of the Great Council's discussions because they involved the entire Five Nations or led to events that would eventually concern everyone.

Alongside this Great Council were the Keepers of Faith and other elders chosen to maintain the moral attitudes and the traditions of the people. Both men and women served in this capacity. The women were also the undisputed leaders of the various villages and residences. Most of the villages were approximately two acres wide, fortified by log palisades with towers and platforms for defense against attacks. Such fortifications were erected on hilltops or on rises, set back from streams so that they would not be vulnerable to floods or to the war canoes of raiding enemies. The clans living within each town had their own longhouses, which were some four hundred feet long and twenty-two feet wide.

Such residences were constructed with sapling frames, tied to form a rounded top, with large pieces of elm bark on the sides, serving as walls. Smoke holes were made in the roof, and there were hearths built into the floors. A central corridor was fashioned by placing two rows of posts down the length of the house, with horizontal partitions used to break up the length into segments for each family. Inside each residence were cooking hearths, utensils, beds, and general living areas. Outside, the family kept corncribs, storehouses, and smoke racks for game. Pottery and clay pipes were fashioned by the women in each village, normally distinguished by high rims. Some were decorated with small faces on them, a religious symbol reflecting the prominence of the False Face Society, a group that performed during certain festivals and were believed to possess great magical powers, including the ability to lure beneficial spirits out of the forest to cure the sick and the ailing.

Kateri's people, the Mohawks, are believed to have numbered around five thousand at the time of her birth, and they had several major towns, each ruled by three chiefs who worked together for the common good. The oldest woman of each village was the matriarch, who governed all activities to the edge of the forest, where her authority ended. The Warriors of the Woodlands, the males, dominated there.

The idea of having women in control was based on the creation traditions, called cosmogony, of the Iroquois people. The Mohawk and their fellow confederation members explained how the earth, the sky, and humans were fashioned by narrating a story about Sky Woman, a female spirit, who was pushed out of heaven. She landed on an island far below, a site created by a muskrat that brought mud from under the sea and piled it in a mound on the shell of a giant turtle. As the turtle grew, so did the island. Sky Woman lived there alone. She had been impregnated by the Earth Holder, another powerful spirit, and she gave birth to a daughter in her exile. This daughter, in turn, was magically impregnated and bore two sons: the Great Spirit (*Tharoniawagon*, or *Ha-wen-ne'-yu*) and the Evil Spirit (*Ha-ne-go-ate'-geh*, the Evil-Minded). In giving birth to this last child, the daughter died.

The Great Spirit then fashioned the sun from his mother's head and made the moon and stars out of her body. He fashioned the rivers, the seas, and the mountains, and then made man, plants, and animals. This creation story, reliant on the equal role of the female in creation, provided the Iroquois with their sense of oneness with nature and all living things. During all this creativity, of course, the Evil Spirit summoned up the vices of anger, war, envy, and other sins, as well as dangerous creatures that could threaten the humans fashioned by his brother. Eventually the two spirits fought one another, engaging in a battle that raged for two entire days. As the Great Spirit proved victorious, the Evil-Minded was forced to flee to the underworld. The evil of the fallen one, however, remained on earth, as did the dangerous creatures he had brought into the world. There were also lesser spirits who worked in the service of the Great Spirit when order was restored. These were beings such as *He'-no,* the Thunderer, the spirit of lightning and storms, and Ga-oh, the spirit of the wind. Many festivals and ceremonies honored the Great Spirit and the various seasons of the year, and the villages participated in these seasonal activities, sometimes sharing a festival with other tribes in the confederacy.

The tribes also shared in war, an aspect of Iroquois life that remained constant despite the united military efforts and the expertise they showed in battle. Neighboring tribes many times attacked the Five Nations in order to gain territory, but such groups were usually repulsed. The Iroquois also initiated assaults, and when they were victorious they were merciless against their fallen enemies. In time, of course, the Europeans would become their major enemy, and were sometimes linked with traditionally hostile tribes.

War was never taken lightly by the Five Nations because it involved forces from all the member tribes, and because it endangered the villages. Once started, war was carried on until victory was achieved. The Iroquois carried wooden shields into battle, and the warriors used tomahawks, an Algonquin word for wooden war club. Breastplates were also worn, made out of reeds and capable of deflecting arrows and lances. The warriors used bows and arrows, tomahawks, lances, and spears in hand-to-hand combat.

The French who encountered the Iroquois in battle said that they "approach like foxes, fight like lions, and disappear like birds." Part of the war ritual, a tradition that dated back to early times, was the famous *coup*, the French term for the Indian custom of daring. Warriors tried to reach a well-defended enemy, creeping into a camp to touch a foe, to mark him, or to slay him in the circle of his own allies. Sometimes a mark was enough to rank as *coup*, but often the Iroquois slayed their enemies in this fashion, which always counted as *coup*. Skill and stealth were necessary in this type of assault, and those who counted *coup* among their activities were honored by friends and enemies alike. This greatly contributed to the Iroquois reputation for bravery, ferocity, and intelligence.

Triumphant in battle most of the time, at least until the Europeans brought projectile weapons to bear along with their overwhelming numbers, the Iroquois were not compassionate to captives. Anyone falling into their hands was tied with leather thongs and marched back to the Iroquois village or outpost, and was normally beaten along the way. At the village, the women elders decided the fate of captives. Some were chosen as slaves and some condemned to die in hideous fashions. The women, even small girls, tortured prisoners, and the torment was designed to last for days on end. The Mohawk honored the war god Agreskoue, and captives died as his tribute, which was why their deaths were prolonged and filled with as much pain as possible.

FESTIVALS OF THE FIVE NATIONS

Village life was exciting, even when the men were not preparing for war and singing their chants promising death to the enemies of the nation. Deeply religious, the Iroquois celebrated elaborate festivals throughout the year, in accordance with seasonal changes and honoring the earth's bounty at different times of the year. Like their ancestors who had trekked across the Bering Strait, these people were at the mercy of nature and its crops. They understood that they lived as tenants on the land, always storing up against the lean, cold times when the snow would mantle the forests and fields with a crippling whiteness. The animals hid in their lairs, and the birds fled the freezing wilderness for warmer climates to the south. Even the nuts and berries froze in the rains and were damaged by the winds, as the earth settled in for months of cold and wet.

The festivals held throughout the Iroquois lands, like those of other Native American communities, were thus related to the natural cycles as they saw them reflected in the earth and in the seasons. Some of the celebrations were listed in the traditions of the Five Nations Confederacy; they were seen as religious and reverential traditions that would unite new generations and bind the entire Iroquois people to the past. These festivals were intended not only as demonstrations of the Indians' gratitude to the Great Spirit, but also as events that provided a break in day-to-day chores, coming as diversions, as grand occasions that brought out the creative skills of the people as well as their good spirits and sense of unity.

The first festival of the spring was called Thanks to the Maple, or *O-ta-de-none'-ne-o Na Wa'-ta*. In most villages it was simply referred to as the Maple Dance. This feast celebrated the precious sweet sap offered by the maple trees each year, a sweetener that was used by the Iroquois women in many ways. The Iroquois used honey, too, but they particularly liked the flavor of maple syrup. The feast honoring the maple lasted only one day, but was preceded by ornate ceremonies. The Keepers of the Faith, those elders who were given charge of the morals and the religious aspects of the participating nations, announced the coming of the festival when the sap started to flow in the maple trees of the woodlands. The celebration was always anticipated by a general confession of sins or wrongdoing by the people.

This Meeting for Repentance, as it was called, was an integral part of almost every celebration held in Iroquoia. A wampum belt, the beaded piece of material that served as a symbol of religious power, as a message during negotiations, or as an insignia of worth, was used during this meeting. In this case the wampum beads were all white, signifying the special purpose of the belt, as the Iroquois believed that anything pure white was a sign of the Great Spirit's partiality. One by one, the men, women, and children of the villages, holding the wampum belt, admitted all the things that they had done wrong over the past months. They promised reformation of character and better conduct in the future, not only for their own sakes but for the good of the nation.

In many cases, the Meeting for Repentance was held in a central location and attended by the people of the surrounding villages. A great feast was also prepared for the occasion by the village matrons, although it appears that the Iroquois did not generally hold large banquets with everyone gathered together. The women of the various clans and families simply gathered up the food for their own relatives and kinsmen and took it to the village or to some distant site, where they ate it in private celebrations.

As with most occasions, speakers addressed the assembled, speaking of the traditional duties of the individual, according to his or her rank and state in the community. Always the people were told about the need to act in common, to live in harmony, and to avoid gossip, envy, and scandal. Orphans, the aged, and the ill were singled out by these speakers, as they had been by the founders of the Five Nations, as individuals worthy of special care and concern. The Great Spirit, everyone was told, watched the good acts of men and rewarded them, especially if the acts were carried out in his name. These sermons were followed by dances, another form of religious experience, and then by games and athletic contests.

When the planting season arrived in Iroquoia, the villages celebrated the Planting Feast, the *A-yent'-wa-ta*. This was similar in most respects to the Maple Dance. During the summer, if the weather was hot and dry, the people held festivals honoring *He'-no*, the Thunderer, at which time the elders begged for rain for the parched earth. The lack of rain was most often viewed as a punishment for some unknown crime by one of the members of the tribe, and the celebration was staged in order to appease the spirit of the rain.

The *Ha-nun-da'-yo*, the Strawberry Festival, was held in honor of the fruit each year. Similar to the other festivals, this one was unique in that strawberries were gathered and cooked with maple syrup, forming a sweet, jellylike substance that was distributed to everyone attending the festival. The whortle-berry, another favored fruit, was greeted with the same type of festival in some regions.

The *Ah-dake'-wa-o*, or the Festival of the Green Corn, continued for four days, as this crop was of particular importance to the Five Nations, and vital to most of the Native American communities in the north and the south. Actually the corn was a type of maize, which was also seen elsewhere throughout the continent. Hardy, easily grown, corn (or maize) not only signified the renewal of the earth and its fertility, but announced the fact that the yearly time of plenty, the warm summer months, had arrived. Corn, along with beans and squash, was called "our life," one of the "Three Sisters," or "our supporter" by the Iroquois.

Tradition held that corn sprouted from the breast of the mother of the Great Spirit when she died. Dances were the normal style of celebration, including the famed and much prized Feather Dance, an elaborate ritual that boosted the mo-rale of the people and joined them to the earth. On the third morning of the festival, after speeches and rituals, the people joined in choruses of song, listing all the benefits they had received from the earth, with the source always the Great Spirit. It must have been a surprise for newcomers in the Iroquois lands to hear the great choir music resounding in the woodlands and the river valleys.

The *Gus-ga'-a*, the Peach-Stone Game, was also played, with each side rooting for their champions. The game was played in a bowl that contained six peach pits. The pits were roasted on one side, to turn that surface black, thus they appeared as black or white when they fell into the bowl. The trick was to jiggle the bowl enough to bounce the stones in such a way that at least five of the pits turned up in the same color. After this and other contests, great helpings of succotash, the combination of corn, beans, and squash, were served to the gathered masses.

The Harvest Festival, called the *Da-yo-nun'-neo-qua na De-o-ha'-ko*, was the last agricultural feast of the year, held after the harvests had been brought in throughout the Iroquois regions. Again, corn, beans, and squash were honored as the staple crops, as the Three Sisters of bounty. This festival also lasted four days, and praised the Great Spirit for his generosity to humans on the earth. The celebration also honored nature itself, the source of all bounty. Dances were performed, and each day's festivities normally lasted until the first rays of the morning sun appeared on the horizon.

The ceremony with the greatest religious significance for the Iroquois was held in midwinter, probably in February, and was called *Gi'-ye-wa-no-us-qua-go-wa*, or the New Year's Jubilee.

The rituals of this feast lasted for seven days, incorporating all the Iroquois religious ideals and all the ancient traditions. Some of the more unique aspects of the ceremonies included the slaying of a white dog and the interpretation of dreams. Like the Maple Dance and other feasts, this one was preceded by the Meeting of Repentance, with special emphasis on the truthful recognition of one's faults and on a true spirit of repentance and reform. Everything was geared to the beginning of yet another cycle in the seasonal march of nature, and to the anticipation of another year of life.

The Keepers of the Faith played significant roles in this celebration, visiting the homes of the clans dressed in bearskins and buffalo robes, with corn-husk wreaths and corn-pounders in their hands. At each residence they advised the people to clean house and to discard trash and useless items in preparation for the ceremonies. The New Year, or Midwinter, Festival was a fresh start for everyone. In a second visit, the elders announced the opening of the festivities and told the people to prepare the wooden blades that would be used to stir ashes in the hearths of the various longhouses as the festival progressed. The white dog, a sacred symbol selected for its pure color and for its lack of blemishes, was then strangled, with care taken that in the process no bone was broken and no blood spilled. The animal's carcass was then hung on a pole decorated for the occasion. On the fifth day it would be burned in rituals.

The second day of the New Year was a time for visiting among the longhouses, and everyone put on their best clothes and went to spend time with their neighbors. The Keepers of the Faith were the first to make these ritual visits, and the houses were opened to the general populace only after the elders had made their calls. Throughout the day, the Keepers of the Faith continued to make their social rounds, coming into each longhouse three times. Other guests came and made the ceremonial gesture of stirring the ashes in their neighbors' hearths. During this time the people thanked the Great Spirit for having spared the households for another year.

On the following days sacred dances were performed, and various forms of the dances were held in different locations. Groups of young boys also went from longhouse to longhouse pilfering what they could. If caught by an alert host, the items were returned immediately; if not, the owners of the various bits of property had to redeem them at the close of the day.

Dreams were also part of the New Year Festival, as the Iroquois, along with other Native American communities, put stock in dreams or visions. Dream guessing was one activity that was popular, as one Indian would go about the village describing his dreams until he received a satisfactory explanation from someone. Members of the False Face Society, the Bear Society, and the Husk Face Society appeared, as did figures called "Big Heads." Games and athletic contests were sponsored, and exhortations were given.

The burning of the white dog ended the feast, and this was a serious and far-reaching ceremony for the people. The Keepers of the Faith and others admonished all gatherings to start anew and to make the New Year worthy of their efforts and their promises. Babies were given names at this time, and the people enjoyed more dances and games. Thus the year ended with rejoicing and with an awareness of the gifts bestowed upon the people by the Great Spirit.

This is the world in which Kateri Tekakwitha grew up.

Films and the various histories of Native American communities seldom explain or detail the very warm, kind, and loving relationship these people had with one another. Indian women especially were loving with their children and attentive to their needs, carrying them about in the elaborately decorated papooses and taking a very active role in their upbringing. In Kateri's case, her mother probably also would have spoken to her about the Christian faith, Christ, and the saints.

On the whole, despite the wars and the torture, the Iroquois society worked well as a structure designed to provide each individual member with a specific role. Everyone worked for the good of the whole. Each man, woman, and child knew his or her place and was well provided for by an extended family.

Vigilance was their strong point always, especially among the Mohawk, who had been given the lands from the Hudson River to Lake George, Lake Champlain, and the Richelieu River. Their lands guarded the eastern gateway to the Five Nations. They had major villages on the banks of the Mohawk River, including Gandaouague (Ossernenon), Gandagoron, and Tionnontoquen.

The Europeans entering the Mohawk domain found themselves face to face with a highly efficient and sophisticated people. The French were the primary invaders in the early periods, though they first entered Mohawk lands as trappers and hunters. Then they arrived as the allies of the Huron and the Algonquin, the hated traditional enemies of the Iroquois.

The impact of the arrival of the European powers upon the peoples of the New World cannot be overestimated. As Margaret Bunson observed in *Faith in the Wilderness*, "the Europeans' presence dispersed the tribes even in the earliest stages or brought about tribal decimation. As the Indian nations moved westward, further disruptions resulted in tribal consolidations or the divisions of some nations. The names of some of the smaller tribes have been lost over the centuries as a result of the chaos."

Enormous controversy surrounds the history and especially the legacy of the European colonial enterprise in the New World. Much has been written about the demolition by the Spanish conquistadors of the Meso-American cultures such as the Aztecs and the South American Andean civilization of the Incas, the severe oppression of the indigenous peoples, and the devastation delivered upon Indian tribes across the Americas from displacement, disease, war, and slavery. Like other aspects of Catholic history, the activities of the Spanish colonial age were the subject of the so-called *leyenda negra*, the Black Legend — absolutely hostile coverage by scholars who advanced propaganda that had its start in the anti-Catholic schools and royal court of England.

In reality, the plight of Native Americans in North America was the source of great concern to the Catholic Church, and missionaries distinguished themselves for their heroic defense of Indian rights. There is no question that European colonialism wrought vast troubles for the tribes and cultures of the New World. But it is unfair to blame the Church for the actions of the European powers who regularly punished Jesuits,

---

Franciscans, Augustinians, and countless priests, nuns, and lay people for speaking out on behalf of the suffering natives. John Tracy Ellis, one of the fathers of American Catholic historiography, wrote in *American Catholicism*:

> No informed person would endeavor to maintain that the churchmen were always in the right, but by the same token no one can deny that they were generally on the side of the angels in their treatment of the Indians. It was the outraged voice of the friar, Bartolomé de Las Casas, which first made Europe aware of the fate that had befallen thousands of the natives in enslavement by the Spanish conquerors. And it was the agitation aroused by Las Casas and his kind that prompted Pope Paul III in 1537 to issue the bull *Sublimis Deus* in which he declared: "The said Indians and all other people who may later be discovered by Christians, are by no means to be deprived of their liberty or the possession of their property, even though they be outside the faith of Jesus Christ."

The authentic approach to the history of the encounter between Native Americans and the Church was expressed eloquently by Pope Blessed John Paul II in 1987 when he addressed a gathering of Indians in Phoenix, Arizona. The pope noted:

> The early encounter between your traditional cultures and the European way of life was an event of such

significance and change that it profoundly influences your collective life even today. That encounter was a harsh and painful reality for your peoples. The cultural oppression, the injustices, the disruption of your life and of your traditional societies must be acknowledged. At the same time, in order to be objective, history must record the deeply positive aspects of your people's encounter with the culture that came from Europe. Among these positive aspects I wish to recall the work of the many missionaries who strenuously defended the rights of the original inhabitants of this land. They established missions throughout this southwestern part of the United States. They worked to improve living conditions and set up educational systems, learning your languages in order to do so. Above all, they proclaimed the Good News of salvation in our Lord Jesus Christ, an essential part of which is that all men and women are equally children of God and must be respected and loved as such. This Gospel of Jesus Christ is today, and will remain forever, the greatest pride and possession of your people.

CHAPTER THREE

THE BLACK ROBES

My confidence is placed in God who does not need our help for accomplishing his designs. Our single endeavor should be to give ourselves to the work and to be faithful to him, and not to spoil his work by our shortcomings.

Saint Isaac Jogues

The third world that intersected the life of Saint Kateri was that of the Church, embodied in the wilderness by the famed Black Robes, the Jesuit missionaries who made their way across parts of North America to proclaim the Gospel among the native peoples from their bases in New France, or modern-day Canada. Indeed, the effort of evangelization undertaken by France represents a remarkable legacy of religious zeal, bravery, and commitment.

The French missions endured for barely a century. They originated in Canada and extended from there to parts of Maine, New York, and areas around the Great Lakes and along the Mississippi River. One of the most significant successes was in the region of modern-day Louisiana. In the end, where the

Spanish missions ultimately collapsed because of the irremediable decline of the Spanish empire, New France's missionary hopes were ended by France's old enemy, England. The clash of empires in Europe spread to the New World, with the future of the colonies, entire nations of Native Americans, and the lives of holy missionaries hanging in the balance.

French (and English) fishermen had long benefited from the plentiful fishing to be found along the North Atlantic coast of America and organized fishing stations in Newfoundland. Soon, French explorers discovered another valuable commodity in beaver pelts. The lucrative fur trade with the Indians only provided further incentive to the French crown. Progress in understanding the extent of the lands before them was made by the French explorer Jacques Cartier (1491–1557), whose expeditions on the North American coast and the Saint Lawrence River served as the basis of France's claim to Canada. Like Columbus, Cartier received royal permission (in this case from Francis I of France) to set out on a voyage to discover a passage to the East. His expeditions, which took place between 1534 and 1541, astounded France by introducing the court to two Native Americans and giving promise of lands and riches.

France in the sixteenth century was roiled by bitter and bloody religious strife between Catholics and Protestants, and thoughts of the New World soon faded in importance. By the start of the seventeenth century, political and religious stability had at last returned, and France looked seriously at North America.

The key early figure for the Catholic Church in New France was Blessed François de Montmorency Laval, the first vicar apostolic and then first bishop of Québec from 1674 until 1688. He fearlessly fought for the rights of the Church in Canada and across much of North America, and served as a member of the governing body of New France. The Church had an important voice in the life of the colonies because of the faith of the colonists, the key role missionaries played in exploration, and above all because the priests who went out into the wilderness — the Black Robes — bore the immense responsibility of preaching the Gospel among the Native Americans. The result was that complaints and demands about the welfare of the Indians found greater reception among the representatives of the French crown than their clergy counterparts ever enjoyed with the officials in charge of New Spain.

The commitment to proclaim the faith was a distinct similarity with Spanish missions in North America. Like the Spanish friars and priests, the French were deeply dedicated to the pastoral care of the Indians and to saving their genuinely worthy souls. This was a reflection in large measure of the same kind of renewal that so thoroughly reformed the Church in Spain in the fifteenth and sixteenth centuries. The reform in this case arrived nearly a hundred years later and lasted from around 1550 to 1650. It was characterized by a genuine rebirth of the faith, and it is not without reason that this period was termed "the century of saints." A few of the most notable and influential figures of the time were Saint Francis de Sales, Saint Vincent de Paul, the great homilist Cardinal Pierre de Bérulle, Saint Jane Frances de Chantal, and Saint Jean-Jacques Olier, the reformer and founder of the renowned seminary of Saint-Sulpice. The religious revival spread from the royal court to the smallest villages in France just as the missions in the wilds of North America — not to mention the Indians of North America — caught the imagination of the French people. The Jesuits, Recollects (or Récollets, a reformed branch of the Franciscans), Capuchins, and other religious orders found many young men and women eager to sail to New France. As with the Spanish missions, the French happily sent out their brightest, best educated, and holiest priests as Black Robes. As far as they were concerned, Native Americans deserved nothing but the best, to bring them to Christ.

The royal crown likewise saw the program of New France in religious terms. Unquestionably, colonial, commercial, and trade ambitions were important, but so, too, was evangelization. Hence, Samuel de Champlain was commissioned, as he put it, to "establish the Christian faith among an infinite number of souls, who neither hold nor possess any form of religion whatsoever." John Tracy Ellis observed in *American Catholicism*, "For a century and a half, Jesuits, Récollets, Capuchins, and the diocesan priests of New France traversed the heart of the continent in pursuit of a goal that often eluded them. If the souls of these steadfast priests had not been kindled by a deep and abiding faith, they would soon have despaired."

White men appeared early in the seventeenth century on the Iroquois domains, and the Five Nations became tolerant of some, and sworn enemies of others. The Dutch started a trading post at Orange, modern Albany, sometime in 1615, proving cautious and considerate neighbors to the Indians. They well understood the nature of the Iroquois and respected their power. The Five Nations had subdued tribes throughout the region and were sophisticated in matters of diplomacy and government. Actually, the Iroquois had expelled the Native Americans living in the Niagara Peninsula as early as 1643. By 1653 they had nearly decimated the Erie and had control of New York and northern Ohio. By 1670 they had conquered the Huron and the Algonquin (called the Adirondack in some accounts), and they controlled the fur trade in New York, Delaware, Maryland, New Jersey, Pennsylvania, northern Virginia, northeastern Ohio, Kentucky, and parts of Illinois, Indiana, Michigan, and Canada. Over these tribes the Iroquois kept close watch, and when problems arose they sent a large military force under the command of chiefs, who gave counsel and took steps necessary to insure Iroquois domination.

The Iroquois found the Dutch circumspect and careful, and they became friendly with the English as well when England took over the Dutch lands in 1664. They traded furs for arms and other equipment and established a "Covenant Chain" that they kept until the American Revolution. The Dutch and English kept to themselves, tried not to interfere in Indian affairs, and treated the chiefs with respect and caution. The Iroquois, in return, treated them tolerantly and allowed a certain amount of trade to flourish between the Europeans and Native Americans.

Not so with the French. To begin with, the French were in Montréal, which the Iroquois called their spiritual or ancestral home. As early as 1609, when Champlain entered the region of the lake that would one day bear his name, the Iroquois took up arms against all French intruders. From 1640 until 1700, in fact, there was constant warfare between the French and the Iroquois. The two groups fought over the Saint Lawrence River, Lake Erie, and Lake Ontario, a region rich in pelts and game. The French were unable to trap or hunt in the area and eventually had to go up the Ottawa River, cross to Sault Sainte Marie, and trap in the Lake Superior territories. This was intolerable, as the infant French colonies depended upon furs.

In order to resolve the situation, the French used Huron and Algonquin allies and tried to manage diplomatic agreements. The Iroquois proved far too sophisticated for the French, who could only offer vague promises and treaties that gave the Indians little advantage. They tried war, but the Iroquois could field large armies and were competent military tacticians who struck terrible blows and then vanished. At times, the Iroquois allowed the French to ravage a particular town or village, staying hidden and untouched until the natural elements and the frustration of never having a decisive meeting drove the French into retreat. In the meantime, the Iroquois, especially the Mohawk, attacked French settlements and wreaked havoc up and down the border between the colonies and the Native Americans. Finally, in 1666, Daniel de Rémy de Courcelles, the governor of New France, led a campaign against the Mohawk in the hope of crushing them forever. The governor and his troops were forced to withdraw after suffering untold hardships in the wilderness. This campaign would be followed by a more significant one, led by the Marquis de Tracy, the Viceroy of New France, with the Carignan Regiment and the French colonial militia in 1667. That campaign would have a direct effect on the life of Kateri Tekakwitha.

~ ~ ~

The earliest temporary French mission in what became the United States was probably on an island in Passamaquoddy Bay, between Maine and New Brunswick, and was started around 1604. The first permanent French colony was begun in 1608 when Samuel de Champlain founded Québec. That venerable city then became the main launching point for French colonization and missionary work. The first missionaries to arrive were four Recollect Franciscans in 1615, followed ten years later by a group of Jesuits. Progress was slow, and by 1627 there were barely a hundred people living in Québec. The brief life of New France appeared to have ended in 1629 when an English expedition marched into French territory and captured the city. Three years later, France was given back its holdings, and new French explorers arrived, but this time with the awareness that the English to the south were going to be a permanent threat, and all too often Native Americans would be used as pawns in the struggle.

At the time there were approximately 220,000 Native Americans in parts of what became Canada (the region stretching from the Gulf of Saint Lawrence in the east to Lake Superior in the west). Champlain had wasted no time in befriending the main tribe in the region, the Huron (the Wendat) to guarantee a perpetuation of the fur trade and to begin forging good relations with the locals. Over the next decades, many Huron became Catholic converts. Champlain's decision had considerable historical consequences, for the most bitter enemies of the Huron were the Iroquois. As the French were allied to the Huron, the Iroquois became their enemy and so, by consequence, were the French missionaries. Initially allied with the Dutch, the Iroquois soon switched their allegiance to the English.

In an act of stunning heroism, Jesuit missionaries set out from New France and made their way into New York to convert the Iroquois. As relations between the French and Iroquois were far from stable or friendly, the decision to set out into the wilderness was a truly remarkable one.

In 1642, the great Jesuit Saint Isaac Jogues was captured with several companions, including fellow lay missionary René Goupil, by the Mohawk. Goupil was martyred, and Father Jogues endured unspeakable tortures that left him terribly mutilated. He escaped captivity in 1643, returned to France, and then went back to the Iroquois as a peace ambassador. Captured once again by the Mohawk, he was martyred near the site of present-day Auriesville, New York, on October 18, 1646. Others followed in death, including the Jesuit priests Anthony Daniel, Jean de Brébeuf, Gabriel Lalemant, Charles Garnier, Noel Chabanel, and the lay missionary Jean de Lalande. With René Goupil and Isaac Jogues, the martyrs were canonized in 1930 by Pope Pius XI and are honored as the North American Martyrs. St. Isaac Jogues died only ten years before the birth of Kateri, in the very village of her birth.

Father Jogues's death served as the basis for future missions among the Mohawks, but the Huron remained a target for annihilation by the Iroquois and the English. From 1648 to 1650, the Iroquois waged a staggeringly savage war upon the Huron, during which literally thousands of the tribe were slaughtered, to the considerable satisfaction of the English. The remnants of the Huron relocated near Québec and finally settled at Wendake, near Québec.

The Jesuit missions nevertheless continued among the Iroquois and finally even the Mohawk. Progress was made between 1668 and 1686, and among the Mohawk converts was Kateri Tekakwitha.

Sadly, at the instigation of the English, the Iroquois once more turned against the French, and by 1684 there were only two priests left among the Indians of New York. In Maine, the Capuchins had started a mission in 1633 at the French military outpost of Pentagoët (modern Castine) on Penobscot Bay. It survived only until the early eighteenth century, when the English destroyed it. To the south, meanwhile, the Abenaki Indians in modern New England made the decision to ask that missionaries be sent to them, marking one of the great stories of Indian Catholicism. The Jesuit priest Gabriel Druillettes founded a mission at Norridgewock, Maine, on the Kennebec River in the 1630s, an outpost for the devoted Abenaki that was raided by the English in 1704, 1722, and 1724. During the last attack, the beloved missionary among the Abenaki, Father Sébastian Râle, S.J., was murdered after refusing to leave his people.

~ ~ ~

The French colonial focus had been centered chiefly in New France for much of the seventeenth century, at the expense of its ambitions in the modern-day Midwest. Alarmed by the expansion of the English colonies, the French crown had widened its interests, and a new area had opened for missionaries. Before his time with the Mohawk, Father Isaac Jogues and fellow Jesuit Charles Raymbaut visited Sault Sainte Marie, Michigan, and the borders of Lake Superior in 1641, and Claude Allouez, S.J., had opened several missions there. From these bases, Jesuit missionaries roamed south and then west into present-day Michigan, Illinois, and Wisconsin.

The European discovery and exploration of the Mississippi Valley was spearheaded in 1673 by Louis Joliet, accompanied by the indefatigable Jesuit Jacques Marquette (1636–1675), who had earlier founded a mission at Saint Ignace on the north shore of the Straits of Mackinac. Father Marquette and Joliet followed the northern shore of Lake Michigan, entered Green Bay and the Fox River, and crossed a short portage into the Wisconsin River, which emptied into the Mississippi. Father Marquette drew maps of the areas and kept a diary of the voyage, some of the most important documents of early American history. He returned the next year to live with the Illinois Indians at Kaskaskia, Illinois, but died a year later.

The missions in the Midwest soon became fertile soil for evangelization. Father Allouez worked for thirty-two years among Native Americans and baptized an estimated ten thousand. The daily demands on the priests were enormous. They made their way through territory never before seen by a European and needed immense perseverance as they followed migratory tribes. The priests were much respected by the tribes, as they learned their languages, dealt with Native Americans honorably, and defended them against the sometimes corrupt fort commanders, fur traders, and soldiers.

Missions were opened in Detroit, Green Bay, and Saint Joseph that endured until 1763 and the withdrawal of the Jesuits from the region. Other work was accomplished by the Recollects as well as seminary priests sent from Québec. All together, French priests and missioners placed footholds of the faith all along the Mississippi.

~ ~ ~

The first French priests reached the Gulf Coast in 1699, and the first permanent French settlement was at Fort Maurepas (now Ocean Springs, Mississippi, near Biloxi), begun by the French military officer and explorer Pierre Le Moyne, Sieur d'Iberville. This was followed by the first parish in modern-day Mobile, Alabama, in 1703. French Catholics began a colony in Louisiana in 1699, and a mere nineteen years later the city of New Orleans was founded.

The future of the Catholic life of New France was, like that of New Spain, largely dependent upon wider events in the Americas, and the dream of a permanent French colonial presence in the New World was doomed by the great imperial struggle between France and England. By 1754, the French and English had fought several wars for dominance in North America. The last was the so-called French and Indian War, waged between 1754 and 1763; it was, in reality, the American theater of the even wider Seven Years' War, fought between 1756 and 1763, which cost over one million lives in Europe. In America, the conflict ended with the English capture of Québec in 1759 and the surrender of Montréal.

By the terms of the Treaty of Paris in 1763, France lost Canada, and the English assumed the task of governing seventy thousand French-speaking Catholic inhabitants. The English government at first refused to recognize the titles of Church officials, hindered the clergy in their work, and tried to install a non-Catholic educational system. Laws were finally passed in 1774 guaranteeing religious liberties to Catholics, but it took some time before actual respect for these liberties matched the legal enactments. The initial moderation of government antipathy toward the Church was partly a result of the loyalty of Canadian Catholics to the crown during the American Revolution and the War of 1812.

The Treaty of Paris also required that Louisiana be ceded to the Spanish empire. In a statement about the encroaching presence of Americans on the region, in 1795 Spain signed Pinckney's Treaty, which granted the young United States "right of deposit" in New Orleans, meaning Americans were able to use the city's ports. Five years later, Spain and France signed the secret Treaty of San Ildefonso, by which the struggling Spanish empire returned Louisiana to the French, although it was agreed that it should remain in Spanish hands for as long as France preferred to delay the handover. As it happened, Napoleon Bonaparte desired to divest himself of France's far-flung holdings to concentrate on preparations for his coming campaigns in Europe. In April 1803, Napoleon sold the massive Louisiana Territory to the United States.

The defeat of France in the French and Indian War all but brought an end to the missions, which had depended upon government assistance. At the same time, the Church in French

Louisiana was buffeted from 1763, when the Jesuits were exiled from New France as part of the wider persecution of the Society of Jesus by European Enlightenment monarchies that ended with the dissolution of the order in 1773. In one of the grim ironies of American Catholic history, the same government that had long encouraged the Jesuits to preach the Gospel in New France now expelled them from America.

The travails of the missions in the midst of the grand geopolitical struggle shaped the destiny of the Church in North America and posed long-term challenges to promoting the reputation for holiness and then the very cause of Saint Kateri. As we will see later, however, the legacy of the saint could not be dimmed by wars, political upheaval, or the domination of much of North America by the English and their anti-Catholic propagandists.

PART TWO

THE LIFE OF SAINT KATERI

Kateri Tekakwitha
April 17, 1680
The Beautiful Flower
that Blossomed Among the Indians

From Saint Kateri's tomb

CHAPTER FOUR

"SHE WHO PUTS THINGS IN ORDER"

People who knew her from her childhood said that she was intelligent and skillful, especially with her hands. . . .

Father Claude Chauchetière, S.J.

Kateri Tekakwitha was born at Ossernenon, the Mohawk fortress called Gandaouague, near modern Auriesville and Albany, New York. The date of her birth is not known with certainty, but one of the best sources is from Father Pierre Cholenec, S.J., whose biographical account of Saint Kateri places her birth in 1656. The year was significant for several reasons. First, it was exactly ten years after the martyrdoms of Saint Isaac Jogues and others. Second, she was born just when the French were regaining the ability to send missionaries into the lands of the Iroquois, an event that would prove of vital importance in her life.

Her name was originally Tekakwitha, or Tegarouite (translated by some scholars as meaning, "she who puts things in order"), or Tegahkouita (translated as meaning, "one who advances or cuts the way before her"). Her father was a Mohawk chief of some prominence, belonging to the Tortoise clan of the nation, one of the groups enumerated by the Great Council at the beginning of the Five Nations Confederacy. The tortoise and other animals and birds, as well as ancestors, served as symbols of virtue, of power, and of special relationships with the spirit world. Some scholars give the name of Kateri's father as Kenhoronkwa, and they ranked him as the war chief of the village and the clan.

Tekakwitha's mother is described by scholars as an Algonquin woman named Kahenta. She was captured during a Mohawk raid on her people, probably in an assault recorded as happening at a place called Three Rivers. Judged worthy of slavery by the women elders of Gandaouague when she was brought into the village, Kahenta worked among the Mohawk, fulfilling commands and performing the usual feminine chores. In time, however, Kenhoronkwa took notice of her, and he married her, giving her full rights in the Mohawk nation. This adoption policy was not common, as a Mohawk did not have to wed a woman captive in order to claim her as his own. The Five Nations Confederacy, however, allowed for the legal adoption of alien people, and the chief took advantage of that.

Notably, Kahenta was a Christian, having been baptized and catechized at the Catholic mission in Québec. This would have been an additional stigma for her to bear if she had not displayed all the Christian virtues. As a Christian, she was certainly different from the other maidens in the Mohawk village. She showed kindness and tolerance whenever she went among her captors, accepting ill treatment without complaints and show-ing a basic good will about her condition. As the other young women liked fine clothes, jewelry, and flirtatious relationships, Kahenta would have seemed ideal for a war chief who perhaps hoped to become one of the great sachems in time.

The infant Tekakwitha would have been carried on her mother's back, wrapped in an elaborately decorated papoose, as Kahenta joined the other women in gathering wood, berries, nuts, and fruits. They pounded corn, brought drinking water from the nearby crystal-clear stream, and hunted down the hives of bees for precious honey. Corn, squash, and beans, were raised in farming plots, along with tobacco. The women tended these plots.

There were Jesuits in the area, but Kahenta probably did not see any of them. She would not have gone to their missions and mission churches without her husband's permission, and he would not have offered it. As the war chief he was aware of the political and military situation facing the Mohawk. The French, along with the Huron, Algonquin, and Mohican, were the enemies of the Five Nations. The presence of the French Jesuits did not console the chief or his contemporaries, per-haps reminding them of the martyrdom of other Jesuits on the same site years before. Eventually, the Jesuits at Ossernenon were warned by their Christian converts and admirers that a plot was being formed to slay them, and the priests left the village in 1658.

As we have seen, the Mohawk and other nations of the Iroquois had good reason to dislike Europeans. The French, Dutch, and English were moving into their lands and proving threats to their way of life. The Jesuits, despite their unique purpose, their dedication, and their love of the people, represented the presence of the white men to the Native Americans.

At the same time, the Iroquois had developed a profound religious system of their own, one that was based on centuries of tradition, from the time of the great migration into the New World. They had spiritual concepts of their own making and an awareness of their place in nature. Many of the older Iroquois, perhaps even Kenhoronkwa, must have felt a certain outrage when they heard the missionary sermons. They must have wanted to delay the inevitable collapse of their world by ridding themselves and their village of the Black Robes. The plot and its warnings drove the priests from the village, and the Mohawks stayed grim and alert, poised to fight against the French especially, even as other tribes within the confederation pondered the wisdom of making peace with the white men and their armies.

But for the Iroquois, generally, white Europeans posed a threat to their stability and their vital relationship with the earth. Many considered the Black Robes the heralds of that threat, turning away members of the Five Nations from their traditions and their lives. Those who converted were seen as traitors to their people and their customs, and were transformed into strangers.

It was a testament to her zeal and love of the faith that Tekakwitha's mother remained persistent in her beliefs despite the hostility of the other villagers, and also as she was surrounded by such a pervasive spirituality. She must have spoken to her young daughter about the Christian faith, and must have taught her children (Tekakwitha had a brother) songs about the Christ and the saints. And Kahenta would have been aware that the Jesuits Isaac Jogues and Jean de Lalande both died horribly in the village in October 1646, and that René Goupil had perished there in 1642, along with French soldiers and with Huron captives, at the time of Father Jogues's torture. These deaths did not deter the missionaries from returning to the Mohawks, and the daring they displayed in coming back into such potentially hostile lands must have won them the admiration, even if given silently, of the Mohawk people. The Five Nations maintained a tense balance with the French and their Indian allies, although the Mohawk, refusing to bend to the whims of foreign white men, did make raids on the settlements near or within their domain.

What Tekakwitha's life would have been like with her family will never be known, as disaster struck her village and the Iroquois lands in 1660. The first sign of the impending tragedy came with the collapse of a Mohawk and the terrible display of the "purples" on his body. The "purples," as it was called because of the hideous rash that covered the skin, leaving permanent marks on those who recovered and signaling the ravages of the disease on the body as a whole, was smallpox. The disease was brought into Iroquois territories by white men, and the Indians had absolutely no resistance to its dreaded toll.

As more people sickened and died, the Iroquois medicine men and shamans performed their rituals, imploring the Great Spirit to put an end to the terrible suffering, but more and more corpses were being carried from the longhouses. The disease struck young and old alike, leaving bands of mourners to wail over their dead. The Iroquois were helpless in the face of this disease. Smallpox did not test the courage of a warrior or the resolve of an elderly matron. The healthiest looking among them, those known for their bravery and honor, sickened and died without being able to summon the physical strength to combat this mortal foe. In time, the villagers became so alarmed and frantic that they began to murder the captives brought home by their warriors. The captives died screaming, even as the villagers gasped out their last in the darkened alcoves of the longhouses.

Young Tekakwitha caught the disease, and she was put on her pallet and nursed by the village women, who despaired of her life. Her mother could not care for her, as she lay dead with her small son in her arms. Even Tekakwitha's father, the great war chief of the village, suffered and died. The village mourned, and the sound of the dogs howling and the women weeping over their loved ones echoed through the woods.

The epidemic eventually ran its course, but its toll had been severe. Tekakwitha recovered slowly, but she was heavily pockmarked and half blind. The sun hurt her eyes and made her cringe and seek the darkness. For a Native American who spent most of her life outdoors, this was a heavy disability.

With the death of Kenhoronkwa, the village matriarchs gathered to elect his replacement, and they chose his brother, named by one source as the warrior Iowerano. A fierce man set on maintaining the old ways among his people, he moved into the longhouse in his brother's place, bringing his wife and an aunt with him. The care of Tekakwitha was given to them, as it was proper for them to raise a dead brother's child, particularly a young woman of such exalted rank. Iowerano appears to have favored Tekakwitha from the start, perhaps recalling the great admonitions in the Five Nations' founding about the care of the weak, the aged, and the orphaned. Adopting Tekakwitha was not only proper, however; it was also a shrewd political move. He did not have children of his own, apparently, and this daughter would eventually attract a fine warrior into the household to carry on Iowerano's lineage. His wife, named by one source as Karitha, welcomed the child lovingly, as did the aunt, Arsone.

When the dead had been put in their resting places, the villagers decided to leave the area. The Iroquois had several ways of honoring their dead, including a special festival in which the remains of previously buried corpses were gathered and moved to a common grave. In this manner the skeletons of whole families were perpetually cared for and never abandoned. The religious beliefs of the Iroquois stated that the journey from earth to heaven took the soul many days. Families often held services at the end of a year, exchanging their mourning cries for rejoicing, as they believed their loved ones had reached their ultimate destination. Later Iroquois lessened the time of the soul's journey. When Tekakwitha lived, the Iroquois captured a bird and freed it over the grave of a loved one on the evening of the burial so that the creature could bear the soul upward to its rest. Most people were buried with their personal things, including bows and arrows, tobacco and pipes, and food for the journey. The body was painted and dressed in the finest clothes, and a fire was provided at the grave during the night so that the deceased could cook its food and be comfortable.

No doubt the families of Ossernenon gathered up the remains of their relatives and ancestors as the village began to disassemble their residences and pack up the belongings of each clan. Ossernenon was now a site of unhappiness, of bad memories, perhaps even of contagion, and the people felt it was better to head toward Auries Creek, to start the new village of Gandawague. All of them prayed that one day new generations would return to this lovely place, to restore it and return it to its traditions. In the meantime, however, it was better for them to start again where the water was clean and pure and where the forests rang only with the sounds of animals and birds.

The move of Tekakwitha's family and clan members to Auries Creek, to the settlement called Gandawague (modern Caughnawaga/Kahnawake Reserve) was a time-consuming effort that entailed many labors for everyone of the community. The longhouses at Ossernenon had to be stripped of their bark and pelts; the poles were removed for use in their new village. The belongings of each hearth family were packed up and carried to the new site, and food supplies were retrieved from the pits and silos where they had been stored.

Unlike the Plains Indians, who followed the seasons and roamed the wilderness in search of game or sheltering havens in the times of winter storms, the Iroquois were normally residents of permanent villages placed in strategically advantageous sites and were constructed with defensive works. Trenches were built around the towns, usually several feet deep. Along the perimeter of these trenches were rows of stakes and palisades that inclined over them so that enemies would be impaled if they charged them. Some Iroquois villages were surrounded by several rows of palisades and stakes. Such fortifications were not necessary in Iroquois territory, where their power had been consolidated and their position made secure. The Mohawk and the Oneida, however, who lived within range of the invading white men and their Indian allies, took pains to maintain fortifications.

At Gandawague, the people decided upon the defensive position — close enough to water yet distant enough to avoid ambushes or sneak attacks by canoes — and the elders selected the best side of the creek and the proper hill for fortifications. Not only were the French raiding Mohawk territories, but the Mohican were also sending in small parties to harass and damage Mohawk towns.

The women of the village, with the help of the men in certain stages of building, were responsible for erecting the longhouses.

Tekakwitha was small and still weak when the move was made, so she did not perform many tasks, though normally all Mohawk children were expected to do their share when the community was involved in a project. As she grew in strength and age, however, her chores increased accordingly. In her younger years she was considered quite amiable and intelligent by her relatives and neighbors, who took delight in her skills in decorating clothing. In his description of the Mohawk lifestyle, the Jesuit priest Claude Chauchetière wrote:

The natural inclinations which girls have to appear attractive makes them put great value on bodily adornments. For this reason . . . girls of seven or eight are foolish and very fond of beads. The mothers, who are even more foolish, spend a great deal of time dressing the hair of their daughters. They see to it that their ears are well pierced, and begin from the cradle to pierce them. They paint their faces and cover themselves with beads when they are going to dance.

Tekakwitha's clothes were stylish and elegant, made for her by the loving hands of her aunts. The women of her clan took particular pride in dressing her according to her rank in the village. These women loved elaborate patterns, and they wore jewelry of all kinds, probably because such finery distracted them from the day-to-day routines. Tekakwitha's hair was plaited and interwoven with small ornaments, and her blouses, skirts, and leggings were fashioned out of the softest hides, beautifully treated and brightened by the use of vivid colors. When the winter months came, she wore a mantle of red or brown wool. Her moccasins were elaborately decorated as well. The Mohawks also wore snowshoes, woven out of bark, reeds, and other natural materials, which allowed them to travel even in the cruelest months of the year. It was noted by her biographers, however, that as she matured Tekakwitha began to prefer simpler clothes, and displayed a reluctance to wear the ornate adornments that were befitting her position within the tribe. She was showing at this early time the humility that became a hallmark of her later life and her rejection of all vanity and pride. In later years, she referred to her faults of youth, and she performed many penances for what she felt was her excessive pride as a young woman. Father Chauchetière wrote:

Katherine's (sic) duties were to gather firewood with her aunt, to tend the fire when her mother ordered her, to get water when those in the lodge needed it. When she had nothing else to do, she amused herself with small jewels. I mean to say, she decorated herself, as other little girls, simply to pass the time away. She put glass beads around her neck, glass bracelets on her arms, rings on her fingers, and ornaments in her ears. She made ribbons and bands . . . from the skin of eels. These they color red and prepare very efficiently for hair ribbons. She wore large and beautiful belts which we called glass necklaces. Twenty years later, when she performed harsh penances to chastise her body, she wept much for these acts, saying she had loved her body more than she should have done.

For a number of years Tekakwitha's life was normal according to village standards, and she was enmeshed in the tender, loving embrace of her new family. She was always sweet tempered and willing to work, although she shied from village dances and festivities because of her eye problems and her disfigured face. Her isolation served as a bridge between the life of the village and the waiting landscape of the mystical soul, where graces were at work within her. Perhaps it was the influence of her gentle mother, who must have remained as a memory in her mind, but Tekakwitha, the product of the American wilderness and the daughter of the proud Mohawk clans, yearned within for another type of life, for another union that was as yet foreign and hidden.

As she matured, Tekakwitha was given many of the domestic duties of the hearth as part of her daily schedule, something that made life easier for her because it spared her the company of young people her own age and allowed her to nurture the spirit of solitude that had become so much a part of her nature. In addition to her duties of bringing water and wood, as well as hunting for small game and for nuts, berries, and honey, Tekakwitha pounded corn for several hours each day, making the flour so necessary to the cooking. She also helped prepare animal skins that were brought proudly into the village by the hunters. She became particularly adept at making headbands and embroidering pouches, leggings, shirts, skirts, and the bags used by the warriors and the women. Tekakwitha also worked on the wampum belts, the bands formed out of beads and shells and used for ceremonial purposes. As Father Chauchetière's account makes clear, Tekakwitha was an active member of the village, but she was always set apart, both because of her appearance but especially because she was different in her temperament and in her disposition to God's will calling her away from the ordinary:

> People who knew her from her childhood said that she was intelligent and skillful, especially with her hands. . . . If I can judge by the objects which I saw her make, I should say that she worked daintily in pigskin and deerskin. She made belts in which the savage women and girls carry wood, and those which the ancients used in negotiating the affairs of the nation, made of glass beads. Another occupation of the savage women

is sewing, which they learned from their own slaves or
from the Christian women from Europe. She was also
skillful in making ribbons . . . from the skins of eels or
from thick tree bark. These she colored red with the
glue from sturgeons which are plentiful among the Iroquois. She knew more than the Iroquois girls, for she
made baskets and boxes and the buckets used for drawing water. Her skill, therefore, was such that she always
had some occupation to fall back on. Sometimes she
made an instrument for grinding Indian corn, sometimes she made matting from tree bark, and sometimes
she made poles for stacking corn. In addition to these
occupations, there were her daily tasks in the service
of the others — grinding corn for soup and bread, and
serving food in abundance. Although she was infirm,
she was always the first to be at work. She spent the
years before her baptism performing these daily tasks
. . . She remained at home and did not go about, nor
was she a gossip. She was neither lazy nor proud. . . .
It has been said that from her childhood she did not
care to assist at the dances or games, and that on several
occasions she had shown great prudence. But she was
timid by nature, appearing only when it was necessary
. . . she could not bear to see anyone harmed, not even
a slave, and she thought it a sin to see anyone burned.

During her formative years, Tekakwitha underwent a Mohawk ritual that was tied to the marriage traditions of the Five
Nations. Marriage among the Iroquois was seldom based on a

sudden passion or desire between two individuals. Most marriage contracts were drawn up by the elder women of the villages, who saw to it that a couple was not closely linked by blood, that they shared rank and status, and that they came from families that would be compatible in the future. Men vied to obtain brides from the better clans, so as to enter them and become part of a higher social strata. Many Mohawk children were espoused at an early age, probably oblivious to the ramifications of the ceremonies when they were dressed in their finery and pledged to one another in the presence of the matriarchs. Espousal at young ages was intended to cement ties between families and to put into place a framework for future unions. However, the children thus betrothed sometimes married one another but could also end up wed to others in time.

In the earlier days, young Mohawk men were not married until they reached maturity, approximately twenty-five years of age, and then many were wed to older women, who served as stabilizing influences. In Tekakwitha's time, however, couples were closer to one another's age. The pairs seldom had the opportunity to discover one another before they were betrothed, as a young warrior could not go up to any maiden and carry on a conversation. Certainly they managed to flirt and to make their feelings known, but marriage contracts were not based on anything as trivial as physical attraction.

As Tekakwitha grew older, her aunts decided that it was time for her to consider marriage. If she had gone through a childhood espousal it had not been recorded. As she neared the age for marriage, the women of the village began making plans. Her physical disfigurement meant very little because she was a chieftain's daughter, the adopted daughter of another war chief, and she was known as amiable, industrious, and talented. When she refused even to discuss marriage, the aunts wondered if Tekakwitha's Algonquin Christian mother had not bequeathed strange ideas to her child.

Tekakwitha did not act obstinately; she did not close the door on the subject, she just put off all discussion of it. The aunts and the other elder women did not debate the matter with Tekakwitha. They allowed her to continue her solitary existence, with its long hours in the hearth area of the longhouse or out in the shade of the wilderness, but set themselves to remedy the situation in their own fashion. One of the acts of accepting a spouse was serving him food. Knowing this, the women invited a very eligible young man to the longhouse, and he came willingly, content that he had received an invitation not only to Tekakwitha's hand in marriage but to membership in her prestigious clan.

After the first awkward moments of conversation, one of Tekakwitha's aunts asked her to serve the young warrior a bowl of sagamité, a type of porridge. Tekakwitha, however, alert to this aspect of the marriage ceremony, rose from her place and went out of the longhouse to walk alone in the woods. There she hid behind a large cache of corn. The astonished young man, refused so bluntly, left the residence, and the women sat and discussed the strange turn of events.

The matriarchs, of course, were functioning in accordance with the dictates of their traditions. They belonged to a people whose safety rested in numbers, especially in the propagation of healthy children who could carry on the nation's affairs. The duty of every female was to marry and bear children for the good of the family, the clan, the nation, and the confederacy. Nowhere was there any encouragement of people remaining virgins. The god of the Iroquois did not request a group of dedicated people to live apart from the rest in order to serve him. Tekakwitha's refusal to discuss marriage was thus alien, strange, and even deemed dangerous to the Mohawk way of life. The members of the tribe were raised to know their place in the scheme of things, and were taught to assume the duties of their station and perform them in gratitude and reverence to the Great Spirit and to the ancestors. The women could not come up with a good reason for Tekakwitha to refuse to accept her role as a member of the Mohawk people.

They were naturally at a loss to explain her peculiar aversion to the marriage bed, and they began to devise ways to bring Tekakwitha to her senses. She had not shown any indication of being Christian, as her mother had been, and she had not talked with priests as far as anyone knew. Since 1658, no missionaries had come into the land. If Tekakwitha was not a Christian, then she was being strong-willed and selfish. If she hid Christian sentiments, she was going against the good of the nation as decreed by the elders. In either case, she had to be punished and made to see reason.

The Mohawks were well aware of the conversions being made among the Native Americans by diligent French Jesuits. Everywhere one heard of the Christian faith and of the havens of Christianity being established in the wilderness. The Christian teachings did not come as alien concepts to the Iroquois, whose own religious ideals prepared them for the fullness of faith. Even chiefs were beginning to discover the faith. Tekakwitha knew about Christianity. She was weaned on the gentle ways of Jesus, the Savior, her inheritance from her mother, and she knew that the blood of martyrs had been spilled in her very birthplace. Now she listened as others spoke of the conversions and the new way of life that was coming into Iroquois lands. If she did not speak of such things to her relatives, it was because of her modest nature and because she was allowing the news to become implanted and nurtured by grace deep within her.

Her refusal to discuss marriage with a young warrior, and her quickness in recognizing the ruse being played on her by her aunts, give indications of an intelligent appraisal of her life and of her ultimate spiritual goals. Her rejection earned her the enmity of the clan women, however, and from that day forward she was to face harsh treatment at their hands. She was laughed at, mocked for her failings, and given the most demeaning household tasks to perform. Tekakwitha was no longer the beloved daughter, the one to be dressed in finery and shown before the young warriors. She took on the status of a slave in her residence.

Faced with such hostility and unkindness, however, she imitated her mother in captivity and met all acts with gentleness and a sweet smile. This attitude upset the women of the clan, who actually liked her, and in time they gave up trying to force her into the arms of some willing warrior. The matriarchs were caught between their affection for this docile, winning maiden and their eagerness to see the Mohawk way of life endure in the world, despite changes, challenges, and disasters.

TREATY WITH THE FRENCH

Events, in fact, took a sudden turn in 1667, when the French forces, under the command of the Marquis de Tracy, attacked the Mohawk domain once again. De Tracy led the Carignan Regiment as well as French colonial militia and Indian allies in the campaign. They burned and ravaged the crops and residences and then withdrew when they met no opposition. The long-term result, however, was a treaty between the Iroquois and the French, with adequate provisions for fur trading, safe conduct, and a general peace. The treaty lasted eighteen years, and it was but one of a long line of pacts and agreements made by the Iroquois over the coming years.

Many of the Five Nations had long considered the prospects of making peace with the French, which would also put an end to the enmity between Iroquois, Huron, and Algonquin. There were certainly advantages in undertaking an end to hostilities on the white man's borders, not the least of which would be a period in which the Iroquois could consolidate their holdings and train their own forces for any future outbreaks of war. The presence of the white man was no longer an issue that could be avoided. There were too many of them, and the Iroquois were becoming vulnerable. It was obvious that these Europeans had every intention of subduing the region around their colonies, and they would arrange such subjugation with or without war.

The Mohawk, of course, had held out against such compromise, having borne the brunt of the French assaults and having the greatest enmity against the white men and their allies. After the 1667 campaign, however, the chiefs among the Mohawk listened to the prudent counsels of others and decided to accept the terms of peace being offered to them. Like the other Indian nations in the region, they, too, were beginning to understand the inevitability of the white man's invasion of their land. The Mohawk region, long held in stewardship and in gratitude by the "Flint-Possessing People," the *Ga-ne-a-ga-o-no*, was becoming inundated by alien people who coveted the forests, the streams, and the pristine wilderness. Like a contagion, these white men were stealing into their woods, across their meadows, and into the wilds. With the others of the Five Nations, the Mohawk consented to a truce that would endure for a significant period, considering the difficulties presented on both sides.

The Mohawk even consented to allow the Black Robes, the missionaries, back into their lands. They did not accept them with much enthusiasm deep within their hearts, because these eager, devoted men represented the inexorable changes that were coming to the Land of the Longhouses. The first missionaries had died at the hands of the Mohawks, and it was perhaps a bit surprising to them that a new group of Black Robes would be willing to endanger themselves.

Three Jesuits, Father Jacques Frémin, Father Jean Pierron, and Father Jacques Bruyas, were blessed by Bishop Laval, accepting whatever fate lay in store for them among the Mohawks and the rest of the confederacy. Their objective was to establish a permanent mission, but until then they contented themselves with wandering missions. This soon changed.

The unanimous decision of the Five Nations' sachems normally held sway and enforced a code of behavior on the participating members. The peace treaty with the French followed that same pattern, as did the return of the Black Robes into the Mohawk region. The missionaries were greeted with considerable ceremony when they arrived. Even Tekakwitha's uncle, despite his reservations, courteously played host to the newcomers. His own longhouse was put at their disposal. Certainly, Iowerano was not suffering a change of heart where Catholicism or the missionaries were concerned. He had deep resentments against their particular spiritual viewpoint, and he distrusted all white men because of the perfidy with which the Mohawks and other Native Americans had been met in the past. The chief was aided in this opinion by his alliance with the nearby British, who detested the French and viewed with scorn the "Papism" that the Jesuits taught. The French, of course, constantly worried about the spiritual destiny of the Iroquois, who were living without benefit of the true faith and the sacraments. Their devotion was so strong, in fact, that they were willing to die in order to bring the "Good News," the Gospel, into the villages of the Five Nations.

The first missionaries blessed by Bishop Laval were asked later about their first encounter with Tekakwitha. They stated that they remembered the visit, especially her modesty and gentleness, something that made her quite unlike the normal Mohawk young woman of the time. One termed her behavior as possessing "a sweet docility" as she carried out the orders of her powerful uncle. Tekakwitha, along with the other members of the household, served the guests, bringing bowls of sagamité porridge and arranging the sleeping pallets and the fires. She said very little to the guests, as she was normally shy and retiring, but she did dare to inquire as to how long the missionaries planned to remain in the region.

The priests probably thought she was showing a courteous interest in their affairs, because they had no way of knowing what was taking place within her young heart and soul. They also had no inkling of the treasure that was present in their midst. She remained hidden, growing in the presence of God and with the graces of the Holy Spirit that formed and trained her spiritual attributes. Tekakwitha had not asked an idle question. She had longed for the sight of the priests, as she had longed for another force to overwhelm her nature.

THE BLACK ROBES

The third world of Tekakwitha's life thus appeared, compliments of the French eagerness to get their hands on furs and lands. Although the Black Robes were French, they did not share in the avarice or determination of their political counterparts among their own kind. They only benefited from the gains made by the armies and the negotiators of New France, enabled to travel at last among the Iroquois and to begin the work for which they had been trained. They were Jesuits, after all, one of the most dedicated and uniquely prepared religious orders in the Catholic Church, who had been drawn by the zeal of Saint Ignatius Loyola and had caught the fire of the early Fathers and burned for the salvation of souls.

The Society of Jesus had been founded only a century before, yet, as missionaries, they represented centuries of martyrs and mystics, saints and scholars, and the tradition of safeguarding the faith in pagan outposts around the world. Such men, and the women religious who joined them in this great undertaking, had maintained the Church through the challenges of the Renaissance and then the anguish caused by the Protestant Reformation and the Enlightenment in Europe. Above all, these Black Robes came armed with the sacraments of the Church, with the presence of Christ, and with the doctrines that would become the framework of a new life for thousands in the American wilderness. If the doors were opened to them by French greed and political cunning, and by the introduction of terrible new weapons of war, the result of their efforts would bridge the centuries again and offer the men and women of the New World a startling vision of eternity.

When Tekakwitha mildly inquired how long the priests intended to remain in the area, her soul was asking for considerably more. They replied that they were there only briefly. As it turned out, however, a chapel was erected in Gandawague (modern Caughnawaga/Kahnawake Reserve) and a missionary was stationed within calling distance of the young maiden. The Black Robes also invested five new missions, a contract guaranteed by the treaty with the French. These missions were started at:

- Tionnontaquen — Sainte-Marie Mission (in the Mohawk capital)
- Onneyout — Saint Francis Xavier Mission (in the Oneida lands)

- Onnontaque — Saint John the Baptist Mission (in Onondaga lands)
- Gayoquin — Saint Joseph Mission (in Cayuga lands)
- Tsannontouan — Saint Michael Mission (in Seneca lands)

Father Jean Pierron, S.J., was stationed in the Mohawk village of Tekakwitha's clans at first. It must have been stressful and difficult in the opening days, despite his love for the Iroquois, as he was, after all, with the very people who had slain his pious predecessors. He was unable to speak the Iroquois language, as there had not been enough communication between the French and the Five Nations to allow the missionary to learn the tongue. In order to overcome this rather critical shortcoming, Father Pierron used his innate artistic skills and his vivid imagination. He painted elaborate and striking scenes and symbols on pieces of linen, visually depicting the truths he was attempting to give to the people. These artistic renditions naturally attracted the Mohawks, who were quite adept at artistic endeavors themselves and were affected by beauty and harmony of design. The presentation of the paintings caused a stir at first and then was followed by what the priest called the game of "From Point to Point." Through pictures and symbols, he demonstrated the progress of each human being from the cradle to the grave.

All of this was rather inventive and astute, but Father Pierron had no idea of the wellspring of traditions into which he was tapping. The Iroquois vision of life and death corresponded to much of what he showed them, and he discovered that they understood a good amount of what he was trying to convey in his performances. The Five Nations had long lived with the view that the human time on the earth was a time of testing for each individual, a time in which duties were to be performed and gifts were to be shared for the good of all. The Great Spirit also symbolized the creative, nurturing, and just authority of a Creator. Such beliefs were already ingrained in the people, thus the exercises proved particularly effective and opened the door to conversion in many.

Father Pierron worked fervently among the Mohawk, baptizing children and the dying while instructing the adults of the villages. He and his fellow Jesuits were extremely cautious about administering the sacraments to mature Mohawks who were in good health, as such conversions not only brought about the enmity of the nonbelievers but endangered the entire apostolate. Adult converts had to be trained over a period of months, and the reception of baptism was a reward for constancy, endurance, and a change of life as well as of attitude. Their reticence stemmed from a fear of apostasy among the newly converted. Apostates in the tribes, those who turned their backs on the Church and the faith when angered or sorely tried, proved often to be the most vicious enemies of the priests. By forcing adults to undergo tedious and detailed catechetical instructions before conversion, the priests also allowed themselves the time necessary to discover the individuals on a personal basis. They could make inquiries as to the moral fiber and the spiritual health of the convert, too. The Indians lived so close together in their longhouses that few secrets could be kept, especially from the Keepers of the Faith or the astute matriarchs. While giving instruction, Father Pierron tried to influence the lifestyle of the Mohawk, constantly urging them to refrain from the use of alcohol, the "firewater" that the English and others provided so willingly. Even Tekakwitha's uncle had to concur with this viewpoint, as he recognized the danger in the use of such substances.

Iowerano, however, was not won over by Father Pierron. He had yet another reason for distrusting the Jesuits and their teachings, and in this bias he was demonstrating the traditional wisdom of the Five Nations Confederacy. Many of the Iroquois who became Christians abandoned their tribes and their home villages in order to live on a more spiritual plane in the Mission of Saint Francis Xavier at La Prairie, on the Saint Lawrence River. The establishment became called the Sault Mission in time, as it was moved to Sault Saint-Louis. There the Native Americans could live in peace, following their Christian ideals and attending the services performed there by the resident priests.

IN THEIR OWN LANGUAGE

In 1670, Father Pierron was moved from Tekakwitha's village and replaced by Father Francis Boniface.

This missionary, adept at languages, became skilled in the American tongues he discovered and was able to converse with the Iroquois. He became more and more familiar with the language as he lived among them, approaching the vocabulary and pronunciation as a scholar. In time he set about translating the prayers of the Mass, the hymns, and the catechisms into the Mohawk tongue. Hearing the Catholic prayers and devotions in their own language had a profound effect upon the people. The Iroquois gift of oratory and the elegance of their discourses and imagery allowed them to recognize the clarity, beauty, and eloquence in another form of worship. The prayers, hymns, and canons that had developed over the centuries in the Church, therefore, had an impact upon them.

Father Boniface also provided the people with a form of worship that was familiar to them from their own traditions. He translated Christian hymns into Iroquois and taught his parishioners how to chant the ageless praises. Every day, in fact, Christians and other curious or interested parties gathered around the altar of the mission to intone the hymns, sending a great paean of joy into the forests and fields. Just as they had sung the songs of praise in the *Ah-dake'-wa-o*, the Festival of the Green Corn, so did the Mohawks join in harmony to celebrate the new faith that had been brought to them. The woods and valleys echoed not just on holy days or on the agricultural feast days, but every day. Many non-Christians were attracted to the choruses, naturally, and they gathered to listen or to sing along with their neighbors. In time, Father Boniface trained a children's choir as well.

Tekakwitha did not belong to that choir, and she did not make herself known at any of the songfests or services. Hidden, distant, almost like a shadow, she absorbed every detail of the new doctrines, listening to the hymns and the sentiments their melodies evoked. There were discussions about the Black

Robes throughout the camp, and the women and the elders debated again and again the doctrinal points that Father Boniface was making in their own language.

At Christmas, he scored a major victory with the villagers. He provided a display that won their hearts — the crèche, the manger scene, used with such effectiveness in days past by Saint Francis of Assisi. This representation of the birth of Christ was totally Iroquois in design and structure, and it bridged their world to the alien one of the Catholic faith. The chapel in which it stood was decorated with pine boughs, pelts, feathers, and other ornaments, and the crib was surrounded by branches, ribbons, and lovely beads. A statue of the Christ Child, the Prince of Peace, was placed in the crib, and he stretched out his small arms from the foot of the altar. The Mohawk came in great numbers to see such a charming sign of Christmas, as they loved their children and appreciated the significance of the infant in the lowly bed of the stable. Such a scene related to their own natural world, and it conveyed the doctrines of the Church clearly.

In this demonstration, Father Boniface hit upon the elements of the Native American aversion to the faith in the past. They resented all things European, even as they might be awed by them, and they certainly did not understand the need for elaborate churches and gilded shrines. They had long felt the presence of their Great Spirit in the natural settings that were central to their lives. This crib, with the Christ Child opening his arms to embrace the world, would have struck a chord in their hearts, as it has touched the lives of countless millions over the centuries. On this "Silent Night," the Mohawks discovered the same spirit of Christmas that transforms the people of the earth once a year into "men of good will" who desire peace.

For Tekakwitha, the Christ Child would have symbolized something far more profound. She was not merely looking for someone to love. She could have found that easily enough in one of the many young warriors of the nation. She was not looking for comfort or ease in a relationship, as she had many offers of kindness and compassion from those around her, even those who did not understand her strange ideals or her retiring ways. Tekakwitha was unique in the fact that she glimpsed, even untutored, the vastness of divine love, and she felt the emanations of that love surging through the wilderness and into her life. She sought the divine spouse, but only because that beautiful Prince of Peace had sought her first.

Whether she was able to spend time contemplating the image of the Christ Child is not known. Certainly, she heard the hymns and the gentle sentiments that washed over the village as the Christmas season was celebrated by the mission. The manger would have drawn her and urged her into the realm of prayer. The decorations, even the image of the Holy Infant, were not the ultimate lures, though. Instead, she recognized the Divine Presence symbolized by the display, and this Presence began to permeate her life. She was already docile, modest, retiring, and unassuming. Now she was discovering that a human soul can be caught up in a mystical embrace in the midst of the common, ordinary aspects of everyday living.

By 1673, Father Boniface had converted approximately thirty adults in a village of three hundred. He was aided in this by the appearance of a remarkable man called the "Great

Mohawk" in his own nation: Kryn. Kryn was a chief of the nation, a convert to the faith, and a man of eloquence and untiring devotion. He lived at Sault Mission, which he described to the new Christians as a paradise of love and faith, where one and all — even those of enemy tribes — could live in harmony and in service to the Lord. The image was quite compelling, especially for those who were devout and experiencing intolerance among their family members and friends. As Tekakwitha's uncle had long feared, some forty Mohawks asked to leave Gandawague in order to reside in their new faith at Sault Mission. Kryn was delighted, and Father Boniface agreed to lead his converts there personally. Afterward, he returned to the village and continued working, but died suddenly on December 17, 1674.

Tekakwitha, meanwhile, was continuing to mature and develop in the virtues, despite her isolation and lonely way of life, and she was already demonstrating some of the hallmarks of truly heroic souls. She remained serene despite hardships, thirsting always for union with God and yet willing to wait until he opened the way for her to come into his arms through the sacraments. Never allowing herself to repay a cruelty with the same spirit, she endured all things and lived as a docile instrument in God's hands, an amiable and pliable approach demonstrated in the past by some of Christendom's most exalted spiritual giants. She was also learning enough about the sufferings of Christ to know that hers were trivial in comparison. Taking the bits of catechetical instruction that were made available to her, Tekakwitha began to set a high standard of perfection for herself, even without the joy and comfort of

111

being able to declare herself publicly as a follower of Christ and the Cross. The Cross, in fact, became her insignia long before she was anointed with holy oils and given entrance into the kingdom of God's chosen.

At this point in her spiritual journey, the three landscapes of Tekakwitha's life had come together — the natural world, the Native American culture of her people, and the overwhelming spiritual power of the Gospel brought by the Black Robes.

CHAPTER FIVE

"YOU WILL SOON KNOW WHAT A TREASURE WE HAVE SENT YOU"

Not only did Katharine practice her faith in such a manner that her confessor declared she never once relaxed from her original fervor, but her extraordinary virtue was remarked by everyone . . .

Father Claude Chauchetière, S.J.

The replacement for Father Boniface chosen by the Jesuits in early 1675 was heaven-sent as far as Tekakwitha was concerned. Father Jacques de Lamberville stands as a representative of a truly unique group of pioneers in the American missions, one of countless numbers of dedicated priests who endured all things for the love of Christ and for the love of human souls. America can boast a remarkable cast of such missionaries, who entered the wilderness, worked there, and died unsung, except in the hearts of the local people. The French Jesuits, the Sulpicians, the Franciscans, the Sacred Heart Fathers, and numerous other priests from the European cradles of the faith, served without complaint to Christianize the New World.

Father Jacques de Lamberville was known to the Mohawks, who named him "Dawn of Day" and "Divine Man." He was born in Rouen, France, and entered the Society of Jesus in 1661. A scholar as well as a missionary, he was one of two brothers sent into the American territories, with Jean de Lamberville, who spent twenty-three years among the Iroquois. Jean was ultimately recalled to Paris to become the procurator of the Canadian missions, thus insuring that a veteran of the wilderness, a man who was aware of its problems and challenges, would conduct the ministerial affairs. Jacques remained always in the New World, serving thirty years among the people of the longhouses. He became the guiding light for the neophyte mystic Kateri Tekakwitha.

It seems as if the controversy over her refusal to marry dimmed somewhat. Mohawk women were practical, and they did not waste time prolonging arguments with obstinate youngsters. Time, they knew, was a great healer, and brought more than one hotheaded child into line. The unique sense of justice that prevailed in the Mohawk community, especially among the matriarchs, also would have soothed the situation. Tekakwitha helped this because she had given no further offense, had not retaliated in any way for the treatment that she had received.

Father de Lamberville took up his post in the village, accustomed to missionary assignments and to the various duties of his role. He was a prudent man, but he was also astute and aware of the great many paths available to human souls in forging their union with Almighty God. His scholarly background and his experience in the field provided him with that perspective.

He did not speak to Tekakwitha for some time. Certainly he must have seen her in passing, perhaps even noticing her standing like a shadow at the Christian festivities. Tekakwitha's life was more peaceful at the time, but she felt constrained and unable to express herself publicly. Then one day, when passing Tekakwitha's longhouse, Father de Lamberville felt impelled to enter. He did not expect to find anyone, as the Mohawk were industrious and did not spend a great deal of time in their homes during the day, although many of the women's duties were performed in their residences.

In a remarkable document preserved in the *Jesuit Relations*, there is an account — written likely by the hand of Father de Lamberville — of the event that followed:

> For several years I did not know her, but one day, having found her in her cabin where she was confined through some foot trouble, I spoke to her of Christianity, and I found her so docile that I urged her to be instructed and to attend chapel which she did with wonderful assiduity after she had been cured. When I found her so faithful I inquired as to her conduct in the cabin; all spoke well of her. In fact, I noticed that she had none of the vices of the girls of her age; this encouraged me to instruct her regularly.

When Tekakwitha saw Father de Lamberville in her home, she welcomed him warmly and began to talk to him of the things that were in her heart. Despite the presence of the other women, she spoke of her parents, of her Christian mother, and of her knowledge of the Catholic faith. Then, without any hesitation, Tekakwitha announced that she would like to become a Christian.

True to his Jesuit training and to his experiences in the American wilderness, Father de Lamberville did not discourage her from becoming a convert, but he did not rush into baptizing her either. He encouraged her to go to the chapel to pray, and it was soon discussed in the community that she could be seen regularly only in her cabin and in the chapel. The alarm of the Mohawk family was lessened slightly by the memory of Tekakwitha's mother who, as a Christian, had prayed all the time, but the conversion of Tekakwitha was greeted as her next departure from Mohawk tradition, coming on the heels of her refusal to marry.

She began instruction without opposition from her uncle or other family members, probably because they felt that she needed something in her life to draw her out of her solitude. Certainly, Christianity was well established in the village by that time, a natural part of the routine there, so there was no purpose in denying Tekakwitha something that others had willingly embraced. Her uncle cautioned her to be discreet and extremely prudent in her dealings with the priests and the other converts. She had considerable rank and could bring about awkward situations without realizing their ramifications or their lasting effects. He did not forbid her to take instruction, and did not make an effort to change her mind, having discovered that she could be as obstinate as he was.

116

Meanwhile, as a wise spiritual counselor, Father de Lamberville urged her to continue in her prayers and in learning about the faith. He had no initial intention of welcoming her to baptism without the usual preparation, no matter how bright and gifted she seemed. She was the daughter of one chief, the adopted ward of another, and as such she carried high status in the Mohawk nation. She needed to follow the same path as the other adult converts, perhaps more so, because she would be an example for good or for ill among her people. He was probably relieved when she showed no disappointment about being treated like everyone else. Tekakwitha appeared for regular catechetical lessons and attended services along with the newly converted Christians.

Kateri thus began her "point to point" studies, having advanced interiorly far beyond that stage, but demonstrating again her unique docility. It did not much matter how she attained baptism and entry into the Church, after all, and being allowed to proclaim herself openly a follower of Christ was worth any delay or prolonged study. Father de Lamberville met with her and explained Catholic doctrine and traditions. He also went about the village making discreet inquiries as to the character and personality of this new would-be convert. No one criticized her character. They thought she had offended custom by her refusal to marry a young warrior, but they could not malign her in any way. She did not have the normal failings of Mohawk maidens, and she did not invite scandal or gossip.

Father Chauchetière wrote:

After Katharine had persevered some time in going to pray as a catechumen, the priest thought of baptizing

117

her. He wished to proceed with the matter, as it was an event of importance to baptize an adult Iroquois, and although Katharine [as she was called by the Jesuits] was so fervent and possessed the qualities of an excellent Christian, he yet moderated his desire to baptize her. On the other hand, he did not wish to defer this baptism too long, for he feared to deprive God of a soul so dear to him. For some days, he made a careful inquiry into the life and customs of the girl. Those of Katharine's lodge spoke only good of her, and the people of the village did likewise, and all the Christians rejoiced when the priest finally decided to baptize her.

Father de Lamberville perceived in Kateri a soul that was naturally Christian. He continued to examine her prayer life and her desire for the faith, and he was soon so impressed that he decided to give her private catechetical instruction throughout the winter of 1675-76. As a result, she advanced swiftly in knowledge of the Catholic faith. By early 1676, Father de Lamberville had decided that Tekakwitha's progress and desire for baptism warranted expediting the sacrament. He announced to her that she would be baptized at Easter. And so, on April 5, 1676, Tekakwitha was welcomed into the Church.

It was important, naturally, and the local Christians well understood the significance of having such a distinguished convert in their midst. As it turned out, the entire Mohawk population had an interest in the ceremony marking the acceptance of the Black Robe religion by a prominent member of the clan. The chapel was again decorated with pine boughs, beads, pelts, feathers, ribbons, and colorful arrangements of wildflowers.

Father de Lamberville named her Katherine, or Kateri, in honor of Saint Catherine of Siena, a saint who was often invoked for women converts. As a result, many Native Americans bore that name, but none would carry it with more spiritual fervor or perfection. When she was baptized, received into the faith, and given the name of the famous mystic and saint, Kateri Tekakwitha was only twenty years old.

Having converted and received the sacraments after so many years of searching and waiting, Kateri was filled with an exaltation that altered her vision of everything around her, one of the most common experiences of the newly baptized. The sky was bluer, the rolling hills more alive to the rain, the forest lovelier and more inviting. She was home, free of the constraints that had dominated her interior and exterior lives, and she was at peace, having found her way into the embrace of Holy Mother Church.

All these reactions are experienced by most converts to Catholicism, whether they distinguish themselves in later years or not. For each, the reception of baptism means the expunging of the past, the rapture of having discovered truth amid so many lies, and the joy of becoming part of a universal family, both on earth and in heaven. It is a plunge into the depths of love and the spirit, so far removed from the halfway measures of many human lives. Kateri experienced these things as part of the process of conversion, and she was now a part of a community of faith that would nourish her and protect her with guidelines for spiritual perfection.

Immediately after her baptism, the floodgates of her soul opened, and she began to seek more and more solitude and to spend extended periods in prayer. The union with the One had begun; she was experiencing a rapturous encounter at last. Father Chauchetière described her demeanor:

> Not only did Katharine practice her faith in such a manner that her confessor declared she never once re-laxed from her original fervor, but her extraordinary virtue was remarked by everyone. . . . The Christians observed her exactitude in obeying the rules of life which the priest had prescribed: that is to say, to go every day to prayer morning and evening and every Sunday to assist at Mass, and (naming what she must avoid), not to assist at the dream feasts, nor at dances or other gatherings. . . . These general rules held for others; but Katharine had done all that before baptism, and so the Father gave her some particular directions and regulated the prayers which she should say and the practices of virtue to live in this manner.

This growing perfection of the virtues to an increasingly heroic degree did not make her particularly popular in the village with the non-Christians, naturally. Perhaps Iowerano and her other relatives had hoped that by becoming a Christian she would settle some problem within her and would become more involved in village life. They had no way of knowing that more and more she was shocked by what she saw around her, saddened by the brutality and the paganism. She had never liked the celebration of the yearly festivals, finding them pagan and often cruel. The ones who had cared for her over the years had not suddenly become barbaric savages, but their concerns about daily life, their interest in the flesh and in pleasures, made them strangers to Kateri as she became more deeply involved in prayer.

The act of drawing apart from her own community marked Kateri as an enemy in the minds of many. Her Mohawk contemporaries, especially the young people with whom she was expected to associate, took her isolation as a form of rebuke. She was setting herself up as a special person in their eyes, drawing attention to her conversion and alienating everyone else. Typical of the young in almost every culture, they could not allow her to continue in her ways without registering their annoyance and their resentment. In some accounts of Kateri's life, these young people are portrayed as harsh devils. It is far more likely that they were simply acting on their innate sense of conformity. They wanted Kateri to join in their activities, to be part of their generation, and to accept their particular outlooks and ideals. When she stood apart from them, they responded the way many young people the world over would respond — with anger, intolerance, and mockery. They were not urged by their paganism or by devilish hatred; these young Mohawk men and women were simply blind to her spirituality, ignorant of the realm in which she was now dwelling, and utterly mindless of her needs as an individual.

Kateri no longer attended the tribal festivals or gatherings, working alone always and entering the woods to pray whenever she could get away. She especially tried to refrain from her normal activities on Sundays and holy days, something that the Mohawk did not understand at all. By doing this, she brought down upon herself the complaint that since converting she was no longer performing her chores satisfactorily. She worked extra hours before and after each Sunday or holy day, but that did not matter and was not counted by her family and neighbors. All they knew was that when she was needed she was not there.

Young people and even some elders began to laugh at her, to taunt her, even to make obscene gestures when she passed. They mocked her as a Christian, a stranger in their midst, and called her as they would a dog. Even toddlers laughed at her as she walked on her rounds or performed her chores. In time, they even stopped calling her by her name. Rather, they called her "the Christian," implying that she had no name other than what she had become. What they meant to be a mocking title, of course, Kateri took as a blessing, for she had lost her name in favor of what she wanted to be — a Christian. They were particularly annoyed by the fact that Kateri was becoming very devoted to the recitation of the Rosary, and she kept one in her hand whenever possible. She had started learning about the Blessed Virgin Mary and about this most efficacious form of prayer. The Rosary symbolized many spiritual concepts for her, and its readiness consoled her as she kept to her daily routines in a totally non-Christian atmosphere. Even Kateri's relatives told her to put the rosary beads away, and, docile as usual, she probably kept it hidden but close when in their company.

Her growing devotion to the Blessed Virgin Mary increased, however, when she was allowed to go with a group of Christians to Tionnontoquen, the Mohawk capital, some distance from her village. There a unique and fabled statue was being installed on the feast of the Immaculate Conception, December 8, 1676. The statue was a replica of one discovered in the trunk of an ancient oak tree in Durant, Belgium, several years before. Depicting the Blessed Mother with the Christ Child in her arms, the statue was exquisite and became the object of pious devotion. Carvers took the wood of the ancient oak and fashioned replicas of the statue from it to send them to other places. One of these was sent by boat to New France, and given at last to the Mohawk mission.

Kateri was present when the statue was installed at Tionnontoquen, and this wondrous event not only added to her fervor but offered her a more profound realization of the role of the Mother of Christ and the virtue of virginity. What she had chosen in the past as an intuitive preference — solitude over marriage, the saving of herself for some great union — became solidly based on Church tradition as a valid lifestyle for her even in the wilderness. She would remain unmarried and alone, thus free to mature in the spiritual life. This statue of the Blessed Virgin depicted the attainment of true union with God, and in the arms of the Virgin the Christ Child once again beckoned to Kateri.

When she returned to her village, probably quite rapt and intrigued by all that she had seen and heard, her persecution increased, reaching the point of genuine peril in time. A young warrior, perhaps the one she had rejected as a young girl, caught Kateri in the forest one day and told her that if she did not abandon her Christian ways he intended to kill her. She is reported to have stayed calm, detached from the violence and therefore more vulnerable. Such an attitude would have brought considerable consternation to the young man, but in the end it would have earned his respect. He fled from the sight of her, leaving behind only his threats. Kateri went on about her business, relating the incident, however, to Father de Lamberville, who was becoming increasingly worried about the situation.

SAULT MISSION

The spring hunting expedition of 1677 proved a turning point for Kateri, as it alarmed Father de Lamberville and added to his frustrations. The Jesuit was aware that it was the established custom for the members of the community to take part in the hunt, but he was also cognizant that the expedition might provide an opportunity for Kateri to be intimidated, humiliated, or worse. He could not protect Kateri from the villagers while she was out on the hunt. He could not even defend her name, because she was chained by the ways of her family, forced to reside at close quarters with them, and was immersed in the traditions and routines of their lifestyle.

Father de Lamberville wanted to help Kateri escape, if possible, knowing that the Christian atmosphere of the Sault Mission would offer her a physical haven and would also hasten her spiritual growth. She had always been frail, and he had no idea of how much more persecution she could take without showing the physical and nervous strain. The kind of persecution Kateri endured was particularly insidious. It was not a violent attack, which the individual can fend off with a rush of adrenaline driven by the overwhelming need for survival. Rather, the daily teasing, mocking, laughter, and cruel insults were like a chain being forged around her and her activities. Each link was small, vicious, and draining, and the priest recognized the signs of exhaustion in her. He marveled that she could conduct herself with such steadfastness and fortitude, holding to her ideals and marching steadily toward perfection.

If he had misgivings about Kateri's participation in the spring hunt, Father de Lamberville could not arrange to have her remain alone in the village. She joined her family in the traditional move to the woods and the open fields, as the Mohawks and other members of the Five Nations had always done over the centuries.

Four months of each year were set aside for a return to more rustic encampments in the wilderness. Basically town dwellers, these days spent in the wilds not only provided the game that would be needed over the winter, but offered the men and women a sort of holiday. They chose areas where the game was plentiful, and most campsites were erected on beautiful hills overlooking streams and rivers. The change of scenery was invigorating for a start, and the routines, quite different from those in the village, allowed the people to relax and share in many community activities. The Woodland Warriors disappeared for days on end, returning with carcasses on their shoulders. The women maintained their normal household routines and treated the game brought in, but they were also able to enjoy the woods and one another's company. For Kateri the expedition proved to be a special time of prayer. She was able to shelter in secluded areas, free from the taunts and the threats. The loveliness of the surroundings also strengthened her and brought her closer to God.

As it was, some of Father de Lamberville's fears were realized. Kateri spent time with her family, naturally. During one particular gathering she made an error in speaking to Iowerano, not using the prescribed formal term of respect. At least this is the story given in the accounts about the source of the accusation against Kateri. An unidentified aunt apparently heard the young maiden address her uncle in a manner that indicated a close familiarity between them. Obviously, the aunt had spent a considerable amount of time watching and waiting for such a sign. She listened, heard what she believed to be an overly familiar tone, then came to the rather startling conclusion that Kateri and her uncle were involved in a dreaded incestuous relationship. This was forbidden by the Five Nations, just as it is considered evil among all cultures in the world, primitive or sophisticated.

As hateful as her conclusions were, the aunt had sense enough not to make her beliefs public. To begin with, Iowerano would have reacted with violence if she brought such a charge. The aunt kept quiet throughout the hunting expedition, but she made Kateri as miserable as possible by warning the maiden that she knew about the relationship and would punish her. The aunt said later that she tried to warn the girl. When the Mohawk returned to the mission, the aunt went immediately to Father de Lamberville to place before him the ugly truth about his precious convert. She laughed with scorn about the "Christian" who had fooled them all. An incestuous relationship would explain Kateri's refusal to marry, after all, as it would explain her uncle's willingness to allow the maiden to stand against the wishes of the matriarchs. The aunt obviously had a twofold plan when she spoke to the priest: She wanted to blacken Kateri's name, and she wanted to make a mockery of the priest's work.

Father de Lamberville, a veteran missionary, asked the aunt what proof she could provide other than a single phrase. She admitted that she had nothing else. He then scolded her for slander, gossip, and evil thoughts, knowing full well that at the founding of the Five Nations such ills were condemned in the covenants. The aunt was silenced, and it is not known if she ever mentioned the accusation to anyone else. Father de Lamberville spoke to Kateri as well, informing her of the dreadful charge. She was surprised, but the accusation probably answered questions she had about her aunt's attitude and increased hostility. Kateri spoke to the priest about the trials of Christ, as her catechetical instruction had trained her in the passion of Jesus, and she said that in comparison with what our Lord had suffered she was only being exposed to a series of minor inconveniences. Father Chauchetière wrote:

> Katharine replied firmly and modestly that she had never fallen into this sin, neither on this occasion nor on any other; and that she was not afraid of being damned, but much more of not having enough courage to let herself be slain rather than to work in the fields on Sundays. She believed she had not done anything wrong by going entire days without eating,

for they hid all there was to eat in the lodge and left her nothing that was prepared for the day, in order that hunger might oblige her to go to the fields, where they would have forced her to work.

These considerations evidenced maturity in the face of ugliness and sordid imaginings. The words of antagonism were bad enough, but as Father de Lamberville realized, they only laid bare the layers of resentment and intolerance being directed against the girl. The aunt was demonstrating the frustration and rage of the villagers. Kateri had risen above them in many ways, had isolated herself in a spirituality that they could not comprehend, and in so doing had invited their attacks. It was becoming increasingly obvious to Father de Lamberville that her conversion would never be accepted as those of other members of the tribe had been. He could only suggest that Kateri pray before the Blessed Sacrament, not to seek freedom from such suffering, but to discover the path that God intended to open before her for her release. He recognized the threats veiled in the accusations. He knew of the young warrior's attack, and he had an awareness of the nature of the Mohawk when they were crossed or threatened. Kateri would die at their hands without complaint, probably rejoicing that she had been deemed worthy enough to suffer such an end for the faith. The priest began to implore heaven for a solution.

The answer to their prayers arrived soon after in the person of an Oneida chief named Okenratariken, or Garonhiague, also known to the French as *Cendre Chaude* or *Poudre Chaude*, which mean "Hot Cinders" or "Hot Ashes." Those colorful images were chosen by the French because they represented the temper of the man, who could fly off the handle into a rage at the slightest provocation. Powerful, strong, and relentless, Hot Cinders was a man to be reckoned with, and the early French learned to walk carefully when in his company. The Iroquois also honored Hot Cinders as a brave, resolute, and honorable man.

Several years before his arrival at Gandawague, Hot Cinders was hunting when a friend brought word of his brother's death. He blamed the French, naturally, and started out for the city of Montréal, then called Ville-Marie, where he intended to hunt down the murderers and take his vengeance upon them. On the way, however, Hot Cinders was informed that his brother had not been slain by the French but by another party. He listened to the details of the murder, thought about the situation, then continued on to Montréal in order to maintain the safety of his people. Hot Cinders had sworn revenge upon the murderers, and if he returned to the Oneida nation, the other chiefs and warriors would be obliged to aid him in his vengeance. War would erupt within the Five Nations, and many good people would die to satisfy his honor. Being a chief of the Oneidas, trained in the ways of the nations and in the ramifications of one man's desires, Hot Cinders knew that he could not bring his people into his private affairs.

He remained in Montréal for the same reason, and in time he was joined by his wife, a woman named Marie Garhi. The pair had a most remarkable marriage. They had been espoused according to Iroquois traditions at the age of eight. They had started living together then as brother and sister, and they had never separated. In time the union was made whole and complete, and the pair remained constant and close over the years, as the result of growing up together and sharing all that life offered them.

Hot Cinders, however, was not the same man he had been when he started out on the path of vengeance. During his stay in Montréal he had been in the company of many he respected, and in the process had discovered the fact that they were now Christians. Learning as much as he could about a religion that could turn his friends into gentle, kind, and compassionate beings without losing their skills in the wilderness or their strength, he decided to accept catechetical instruction. The missionaries in Montréal also practiced the custom of making converts of adult age take weekly classes and prove themselves worthy of baptism. Hot Cinders, naturally, brought all the force of his personality into his conversion, forging anew his honor, his courage, and his mental prowess in the changes taking place. When baptized he was given the name Louis, after Saint Louis, king of France, that gentle and ascetic ruler, and he became an exemplary member of the Christian community.

He attended two Masses a day, received holy Communion, was especially devoted to the Blessed Sacrament, and conducted his affairs with calm. Word of his conversion naturally spread across Iroquoia, and his former warrior companions made the long trek to Montréal to discover for themselves what had taken place. They were quite stunned to find Hot Cinders spreading the doctrines of Christianity, but they listened attentively, drawn as usual by his fiery eloquence.

It is difficult for modern Catholics to understand the remarkable impact that the faith had upon the Iroquois nation and its leaders. Certainly the ideals and spiritual concepts of the Native Americans prepared them for the profoundly beautiful aspects of Christianity, and their sense of obligation and honor fitted them admirably for carrying out the commands of Christ throughout their lives. They came to the Church with a unified purpose, with strength tested in the wilderness, and with a basic wisdom about the earth and mankind that fortified their beliefs. Certainly not every Iroquois was a magnificent specimen of the faith, as that does not happen in any land, but the early converts were great enough to cause a sensation among their own people.

After discussing the situation, the Oneida elders went to Hot Cinders and asked him to return as their chief. He could practice his faith, instruct others, and fulfill whatever he believed to be his destiny as a Christian. The former chief, however, recognized the dangers of his returning to the wilderness and set about making a series of proposals that he knew his own people would not be able to accept in good faith. First he demanded that all the Oneidas in his tribe become Christians. That was very difficult for them, because not all of them had been convinced of the need to put aside their traditional spirituality. Even more of them might have considered making a conversion, but the Church represented not only Christ and the saints but the white men, particularly the French. They balked at this, but did not actually refuse to accept the first condition. Hot Cinders, therefore, made his second demand, which he knew would put an end to all negotiations about his return.

He insisted that the Oneidas abandon their tribal lands and live in the Sault Mission. This was impossible, and he knew that as well as they did. The Oneidas would never give up their ancestral lands, not even for Hot Cinders and his new faith. Such a move would not only put them at the mercy of the white men, but would allow others to intrude and slowly engulf the lands of the People of the Stone, the *Ona-yota-ka-o-no*. The elders sadly bade Hot Cinders goodbye and went away, wondering what sort of power had overtaken their leader. A resolute Hot Cinders maintained his Christian ways and led a very distinguished life, becoming chief of Sault Mission in time. He was slain in 1684 in a war with the Senecas.

In Kateri's time, however, he not only administered Indian affairs at Sault Mission but went on journeys throughout the Iroquois territories, accompanied by trusted friends. He and Kryn, the "Great Mohawk," visited the various villages of Iroquois to talk to their people about the faith. Eloquent orators, the two men spent days on the trails, stopping to gather the members of the Five Nations so that they could explain their conversion and the beauty of the Church in their lives. The two famed leaders reached far more Indians than the missionaries could, and they were able to explain the Catholic faith in terms that were far more reasonable and enticing.

In 1677, accompanied by a Huron from the Mission of Lorette and by a relative of Kateri, Hot Cinders arrived in Gandawague to speak to the Catholic converts and to address the villagers. As it happened, his visit came at a time when Kateri's uncle was away from the village on a visit to a nearby Dutch fort. The Huron was some kind of a relative to Kateri, perhaps her brother-in-law, married to Kateri's half-sister. In some versions of Kateri's life, her uncle adopted a second daughter. Nothing is known of the woman's life as a child, however, and she is only casually identified as Kateri's half-sister in later biographies. When the two men arrived in the village they went straight to the chapel. There they were greeted with joy by Father de Lamberville, who considered them angels from God. Hot Cinders brought with him a catechetical tapestry, the beautifully colored illustration of Christian life that served as a *Do giquese*, a catechist, to the people. When the tapestry was raised up in a village, the people came to listen to the talks and to ponder the power of the faith that could attract such eloquent and gifted veterans of life. Kateri listened to their words, and in her heart she knew that they had been sent to Gandawague as her release.

She knew that the men were stopping over just for a few days. She approached them and asked if there might be some way for her to journey with them. Hot Cinders, who had been made aware of the problems in the village, readily agreed. He was setting out immediately on his own for the lands of the Oneida to preach among the Iroquois, but she would be a welcome member of the party that was heading back to the Sault Mission. With great haste and in the dark of the night, Kateri gathered up her belongings and met with her new traveling companions. With no fanfare or long goodbyes, Kateri left the home she had known for almost her entire life.

As sorry as he was to see her go from his charge, Father de Lamberville advised Kateri to go. He then sat down at his desk and wrote a letter to the priests of Sault Mission to alert them to Kateri's special needs and potential. Kateri, the Huron, and her relative set off in one canoe, as Hot Cinders paddled in the opposite direction. Just how many people in the village saw them leave is not known, but the cry went up a short time later when it was discovered that Kateri was gone, and that the three men were gone as well. A discussion was held in Gandawague, and then a runner was sent to Iowerano with the dire news. The uncle was furious at what he believed was a kidnapping or a planned escape, and hurried back to the village. He took up his gun and loaded it with three bullets, as if he expected to slay the three men before dragging Kateri back to his longhouse. He must have given Father de Lamberville a very difficult time as well, blaming him for the loss of his niece and adopted daughter.

Meanwhile, the fugitives, having paddled some distance, had split up temporarily, as the Huron made his way to the Dutch settlements, hoping to beg some bread there. This lack of supplies indicates that the departure from Gandawague was hurried and in secret. The Huron directed his canoe toward the Dutch and found himself in the path of Kateri's uncle, who was paddling furiously in search of the escapees. As the uncle did not know the Huron by sight, being away from the village during the man's brief stay there, he passed him without a word. The Huron, however, doubled back quickly and alerted Kateri and her relative. They moved away from the river, and the Huron fell back as a rear guard. Iowerano was a superb paddler and tracker, and surely would soon be visible coming behind them. Kateri and her relative raced along the forest trails, trying to put some ground between them and the stalking war chief of Gandawague.

The uncle did appear, as the Huron had expected, and so he fired a shot into the air to warn the others, then set about beating the bushes as if looking for game. Iowerano did not recognize the Huron as the man he had seen on the river, and raced past him farther into the woods, where he came across another Indian, sitting calmly by the side of the trail, smoking. This was Kateri's relative, who had hidden her carefully and then had staked out a position that was quite obvious and therefore deceptive. The uncle had never laid eyes on this man before either, so he stalked off, still looking for his prey. He continued searching for several hours, covering vast tracts of land, but then he gave in to his frustrations and made his way back to Gandawague, knowing that Kateri was lost to the village forever.

This uncle is a pivotal figure in the early life of Kateri Tekakwitha, but remains somewhat of an enigma, shrouded in his duties and in his command position in the clans. Certainly he was a man of considerable compassion and concern, as evidenced by his adoption of Kateri and perhaps of a second daughter. He also showed that he honored his brother's memory in this act, but the care of orphans and others weakened or made vulnerable by tragedy was an Iroquois hallmark. They showed no such mercy to outsiders who fell as victims into their hands. Then, of course, their fates were sealed by the matriarchs, and their deaths, hideous and prolonged, came at feminine hands. The uncle's anger over the flight of Kateri was probably prompted by several motives, the loss of his prestige being paramount. He was a chief, used to being obeyed by those under his command, and certainly this maiden had defied him over the decades. He also sought her out of affection as well, determined to drag her back and to make her conform to the Mohawk traditional roles, if for no other reason than to insure her safety and her ultimate happiness. As it was, he disappears from the scene forever, and nothing is known of his life with certainty after that last dreadful hunt through the forest.

The Christians bent on seeing Kateri safe and sound at Sault Mission managed to elude the stalker and began their journey in earnest. They probably carried their canoe to the Hudson River, where they could paddle up to Jessup's Landing, crossing then to Luzerne in the north and on to Lake George, then called Lake Saint Sacrament. There the canoe, which had been hidden carefully by Hot Cinders at the start of the journey, was used to cross into Lake Champlain. From there the route led to the Richelieu River and then to the Sault Mission, which Kateri reached in the autumn of 1677. She had retraced the steps of her Christian mother, who had been taken from the mission into the wilds, captured, and then dragged into the Mohawk realm. Kateri said later that her joy increased with each mile they covered in the wilderness. Certainly her companions, tried and tested Christians, must have seemed like angels to her, as they carried on the daily prayer rituals ingrained in them by their catechetical training and by their lifestyle in the Christian missions. Although they moved through the rugged wilderness, which was dangerous because of hostile tribes and animals, they kept the spirit of Christ alive in their hearts. Kateri was entering a paradise of sorts, a site devoted to all the spiritual ideals that had taken hold of her heart and soul. She did not anticipate being free of suffering there, as she was wise already in the way of the Holy Cross, but at least she could serve the Church and Christ without being terrorized by her family and neighbors. Father Chauchetière wrote:

> Behold the Genevieve of Canada, the treasure of the Sault who had sanctified the roads between the Mohawks and Montréal, along which many chosen souls have passed after her. When she found herself far from her own country and realized that she need no longer fear her uncle, she gave herself entirely to God, leaving the future in His hands. She arrived in autumn of 1677, having made an uninterrupted journey because of her great longing to reach her destination. . . . It is impossible to portray the joy she experienced in being in the land of sunshine, freed from the anxiety she had felt at not being able to serve God as she wished, in being released from the persecutions she had endured in the lodge in her own country, in having holy companions, and in being able to hear several Masses a day, and above all in being able to receive holy Communion frequently.

Kateri carried with her the letter from Father de Lamberville, directed to the pastors of the mission, Father Jacques Frémin, and his assistants, Father Pierre Cholenec, a Jesuit from Brittany, France, a devoted, amiable man, and Father Claude Chauchetière, who is also mentioned in the records. The letter introduced Kateri, and in it Father de Lamberville advised them that Kateri "is going to live at the Sault. Will you kindly undertake to direct her? You will soon know what a treasure we have sent you. Guard it well then! May it profit in your hands, for the glory of God and the salvation of a soul that certainly is very dear to him."

CHAPTER SIX

"A SAINT AMONG THE JUST"

Her soul was well disposed toward perfection; and throwing her-self into this with singular devotion, she adopted all the practices which she saw were good. . . . It was only a matter of a few weeks until she stood out among all the other women and girls of the mission . . . in a short time, a saint among the just and faithful.

Father Pierre Cholenec, S.J.

The mission that welcomed Kateri and her companions at the end of their long and arduous journey in October 1677 had originally been built at the southern end of La Prairie, near Ville-Marie, or Montréal. That site had been recognized almost immediately as ill chosen. The soil was bad, discouraging the farming occupations of the converts and making their food rations short. At the same time, the mission was too close to the various French settlements. This proximity involved the

Christian Native Americans in French affairs, which benefited them by introducing them to European ways, but also made them subject to the bigotry, intolerance, and general cantankerousness of the local French settlers. The Jesuit priests normally maintained a distance from their own kind in establishing their missions, isolating the new converts to a degree in order to shelter them and prevent unnecessary interference from the French colonial population and its diseases and temptations, especially alcohol.

The king of France, Louis XIV, solved the problem by granting a new territory to the Jesuits. He provided them with a site at Sault near La Prairie de la Madeleine, three to four miles upriver from La Prairie, where the Portage River emptied into the mighty Saint Lawrence. On a wide plateau that resulted from the joining of these two waterways, the mission was ideally situated, both from a scenic and a fortifications standpoint. In front of the complex was the beautiful Lake Paul, and in the distance were Ville-Marie and Mount Royal. On the left was Heron Island, surrounded by azure water, standing isolated and starkly profiled against the horizon at the foot of the rapids. The mission was called Saint Francis Xavier of Sault Saint-Louis. Sault translates from the French as rapids.

The thinking involved in the land grant by King Louis XIV, of course, did not strike any of the priests or the French court. In granting lands to the Jesuits, as to everyone else who received land from him, King Louis XIV did not recognize its present or previous owners. It was assumed by the white men that the king owned all the lands in that part of North America, and therefore was merely exercising his royal rights in order to provide the Jesuits with a needed site. The fact that the land was already occupied — and had been for centuries — by Native American tribes, had no impact upon the Europeans' acquisition and distribution of land tracts in the wilderness of the New World. As Spain acted in the southern regions of the continent, so France, England, and the Dutch accumulated land in the northern territories of the continent and used them as they saw fit. No one discussed the moral or legal ramifications of such possession or use. The Native Americans were mere spectators in the division of North America, as their counterparts died from disease and mistreatment in Mesoamerica and in the realm of the Incas in South America.

The Mission of Saint Francis Xavier of Sault Saint-Louis was composed of a chapel and adjoining work areas and residences for the priests stationed there. The complex was surrounded by a stout stockade. The cabins of the Christian Native Americans were built outside these defensive walls, and there was an advantage to their independence. The Spanish brought their converts inside the main walls of the missions, most of which were rather large and commanding. The Native Americans were thus brought into contact with European customs by force, and they were allowed to govern themselves only to a point. The French priests preferred to allow the Native Americans to conduct their own affairs, providing only a sheltering spiritual haven. In case of attack, the converts could come within the walls for safety. Father Chauchetière wrote in 1682:

We are in a very high and beautiful location, with a fine view, 60 leagues distant from Québec, which is

THE LIFE OF SAINT KATERI

called "the Iroquois mission." It is the finest mission in Canada, and as regards piety and devotion, resembles one of the best churches in France ... we have a chapel 25 feet wide, and nearly 60 feet long. We have three bells, with which we produce a very agreeable carillon; and the savages will soon have another bell, weighing two hundred *livres*, to complete the harmony.

Standing on a rise, surrounded by forests, streams, Lake Paul, and the splendor of the countryside, Sault Mission housed an Indian population of between one hundred twenty and one hundred fifty, residing in sixty cabins. Their lives were much like the ones they had led in their home villages, with the usual farm labors, gathering in the fields, hunting, and household chores. The Indians moved into wilderness campsites during the year for the annual hunt, which provided game for their larders and allowed them to be free, for a time, of any restraints imposed by the proximity of the Europeans.

The setting of the mission — in the wilderness that the Indians knew and reverenced as part of the divine plan for all humans — offered the converts to the faith a perfect and isolated stage upon which their spiritual development continued without interruption. With men like Kryn and Hot Cinders available to them, urging them forward and reinforcing Christian doctrines, the people existed as a rare Christian community in the wilds. Hot Cinders spoke to them eloquently of Christ, of the barbaric nature of their past, and of the joys awaiting each soul who clung to Christ and his Cross.

The piety that resulted, and the unstinting manner in which the Christian Indians lived in commune, astounded the white men and women who came into contact with them. Rumors about Sault Mission spread throughout New France, and many came to visit the chapel, to speak to the priests, and even to participate in the religious services. They left edified by the example the Indian converts set for others. Informed of the situation at the mission, Bishop Jean-Baptiste de Saint-Vallier of Ville-Marie, also went to see for himself. He had believed the rumors about the piety and spirituality to be quaint and rather exaggerated, but his short stay among the Iroquois taught him that they had ascended to another level of Christian participation, and he reported that everything said of these converts was true. In time, the local French attended services at the mission chapel, not to sit and gape at the converts, but to share in grace and in the faith with these dedicated fellow Catholics.

The daily routine of the Native Americans was made up of traditional Native American life interwoven deeply with the Catholic faith. The village was thus filled with the sounds of Indian families at their daily labors, interspersed with the great tolling sound of the mission bell that set the schedule for religious services and for prayers. Even the *Angelus* was rung on that bell, echoing out across the fields and the forests. The Christian Indians would halt their labors to recite the lovely greeting to Our Lady, echoing in the New World the same prayers being said in countless communities across the earth. They were one with the white men, not in progress, not in civilizing efforts, but in the true vocation of all human beings, in the affairs of the spirit.

One of the most remarkable aspects of Sault Mission was its diverse population. Members of tribes that had enmity or hostility to one another throughout the decades lived there side by side. The very tribes that had warred on one another in the past now laid aside their rivalries and feuds in the name of Christ. Using the strengths of the Indian people as a whole, the converts bound themselves as one in the name of Catholicism. They were the bearers of Christ's light in the wilderness, and as such they conducted themselves with kindness, humility, and incredible fortitude.

In a letter from Father Cholenec to a fellow Jesuit, Father Le Blanc, in 1715, he described the conditions at the Sault:

> The example and devotion of these new converts drew to them many of their countrymen, and in a few years the Mission of Saint Francis Xavier of the Sault (for thus it is named), became celebrated for the great number of its neophytes and their extraordinary fervor. Iroquois who visited the Sault, even if for a brief stay with relatives or friends, seemed to lose all desire of returning to their country. The charity of these neophytes led them even to share with these newcomers the fields they had cleared with much labor. But the way in which this feeling appeared to the greatest advantage was in the eagerness they showed in instructing them in truths of our Faith. To this work, they devoted entire days and even a portion of the night. Their conversations, full of unction and piety, made the most lively impression on the hearts of their guests,

and transformed them, so to speak, into different beings. He who a little while before breathed nothing but blood and war, became softened, humble, tractable, and ready to obey the most difficult maxims of our religion.

This zeal did not restrict itself to those who came to visit them, but induced them also to make excursions into the different settlements of their nation, and they always returned accompanied by a large number of their countrymen.

New Life

At the time of Kateri's arrival, the missionary leadership of the village consisted of three Jesuits: Father Frémin, a Jesuit Black Robe of long experience; Father Cholenec, who had been at the mission for several years; and Father Chauchetière, who had arrived several months before. All three had the opportunity to welcome Kateri to the settlement and then to get to know her in the coming years. They also left to history a number of accounts of her life and her holiness. Father Frémin initially took charge of her continued catechetical instruction and spiritual direction, but soon gave the responsibility to Father Cholenec.

When Kateri arrived in this haven, it was decided that she would live with her relatives, the man who had escorted her from her village, and his wife. This is the woman who is sometimes called Kateri's half-sister, but she was not related to her in any physical sense. She may have been the second daughter adopted by Iowerano, a woman who had married and had followed her husband to the mission. Such a view poses a severe and obvious problem, of course. Kateri's uncle would certainly have recognized a son-in-law on the trail in the forest. He is depicted in the accounts as passing him by, thinking him to be just another Indian smoking while taking a brief rest from hunting. The man was probably related to Kateri on her mother's side, a stranger to Iowerano and the other Mohawks of the village.

Kateri was welcomed warmly into their cabin, where lived as well an older woman named Anastasia, who had been a close friend of Kateri's mother before she was captured and taken into the Mohawk lands. She was delighted to discover the child of her past companion and opened her arms and her heart to Kateri. The Jesuit priests noted the joy that Kateri had in the community. According to Father Cholenec, she was "edified exceedingly" by the piety of the converts at the mission, and she was impressed especially by the virtue of the men, whose behavior was in stark contrast to the life they had led in their villages.

In the house and in the fields, Kateri set about earning her place in the community, showing the same willingness and fidelity that had distinguished her even in the times of persecution among her own. She was coming to life, stunned by the beauty of the mission site and by the angelic atmosphere of the city. The life of the mission was certainly conducive to her spiritual development, and all the graces and spiritual ideals that had blossomed unseen for so many years began to bloom at the Sault.

The Jesuits maintained strict control over religious services and practices, never allowing themselves to slack or lessen their obligations. Each day started at 4:00 a.m., as the last stars were fading in the night sky and the forests lay mantled beneath the mists and the chill of the early hours. In that stillness, in that moment of hushed beauty, the priests rose to say the Divine Office, the Breviary, as it was recited in monasteries and convents throughout Europe. This recitation confirmed the religious vocations of the priests and united them in spirit with the Church in the world. The mission bell was rung at that hour, alerting the local Indian Christians, who rose and made their way to the chapel or began their private devotions in their cabins.

Two Masses were celebrated each morning, the first after recitation of the Divine Office, and another at 8:00 a.m., attended by the congregation. Many of the locals were at the first Mass as well. Kateri learned quickly that the Mass was open to her, and she began her day with the first bell. These Masses were quite unique in that they were accompanied by chants in the Iroquois language, sometimes in full harmony, as in the festivals of the Mohawk and other tribes of the Five Nations. Again the wilderness resounded with harmony, as human voices were raised to greet the first light of each day and to give praise. The sermons were often preached by Iroquois leaders. Their eloquence stirred the congregation and urged them to greater spiritual perfection. A Rosary often followed the Masses, and the people returned throughout the day to meditate and pray before the Blessed Sacrament in the chapel.

After the first Mass, Kateri remained in prayer until the city Mass at 8:00 a.m., which was preceded by the Sacrament of

Confession. During this second Mass the men sat on one side and the women on the other. There was also a special group of converts, members of the Brotherhood of the Holy Family, a pious association devised by the Jesuits to honor the more advanced among their converts and to bring a stabilizing, spiritually oriented continuity to the mission congregations. Only the finest among the converts were admitted to this association, and they took their responsibilities and their honors seriously. The Brotherhood served as a counterpart to the traditional Keepers of the Faith in many ways, maintaining the moral tone of the congregation and exercising wisdom in Indian affairs. The freedom that the Native American communities had in the Jesuit missions hastened the independent efforts of each man and woman to advance spiritually. This is not to say that each person in the Iroquois Christian communities reflected the highest virtues or epitomized the saintly. Most human beings, whether Native American, white, or otherwise, do not aspire to the same levels of spiritual growth. Some are born with limited capacities for learning, for self-rule, or for personal development. Some are gifted but not prone to exercising the sort of heroic efforts necessary for the perfection of the virtues. The same variations surely existed at Sault Mission, but the distinguishing hallmark of the congregation living there is the effort made by one and all to achieve a peaceful, grace-stimulating world in which a young person such as Kateri could flower easily. This reflects once again the great vision of the Tree of Peace at the founding of the Five Nations, where men and women living in the wilds of the New World banded together to bring harmony, cooperation, and peace to their domains.

The Brotherhood of the Holy Family met each day at 1:00 p.m., when the members recited prayers and discussed mission affairs. At 3:00 p.m., the entire congregation joined the Brotherhood at Vespers, the beautiful Divine Office that not only closes the liturgical themes of each day but anticipates the festival to be celebrated on the morrow. The congregation chanted psalms that Father Frémin had translated into Iroquois, using the monastic tones. The service normally ended with Benediction of the Blessed Sacrament.

Kateri's devotions, and those of the more pious Christians of Sault, did not revolve solely around the scheduled religious services in the chapel. Even the local landscape offered the wise places of meditation and contemplation. On the banks of the river a gigantic cross had been raised. Unrestrained by the forces that had made her life so difficult in her village, Kateri used the chapel services and the natural loveliness of her surroundings to practice the Christian ideals that had formed in her heart in secret for so many years. She also listened, watched, and imitated the calm, serene, and highly devoted individuals at the mission. Father Cholenec described her in the early days, saying that she almost burst with happiness in being in such an atmosphere of prayer and grace. He added:

> Her soul was well disposed toward perfection; and throwing herself into this with singular devotion, she adopted all the practices which she saw were good. . . . It was only a matter of a few weeks until she stood out

among all the other women and girls of the mission . . .
in a short time, a saint among the just and faithful.

Retiring as always, normally keeping her head covered
with a shawl, Kateri chose the companionship of Anastasia,
which was a normal thing to do. This woman was not only
wise in the ways of the mission and the Christian life, but she
was a link to Kateri's past. Anastasia could sit for hours talking
about Kateri's mother and about the saints. The older woman
slowly introduced her to the practices held in common in the
mission, but she offered her advice on appearance, demeanor,
and attitudes as well.

The attitude of most of the Christian Indians was one of
remorse and repentance, particularly among those who had
converted late in life. Such remorse for the past was the result
of their recognition of grace, of unique opportunities, and of
the customs which they had practiced before their conversions.
Many had taken part in the barbaric cruelty to war prisoners
and slaves, and perhaps even in the ritualized slaying of the enemy. Men and women had shared in the atrocities, as they had
participated in drunken sprees and in immoral relationships.
They looked back on such things with horror and with sorrow,
particularly as the faith introduced them to the beautiful ways
of Christ and to the spiritualization of existence.

Kateri, seeing this genuine remorse and listening to the
grief the converts exhibited, followed their lead and repented
of her own past. The fact that she had never allowed herself to
take part in the barbaric traditions of her own people, customs
that she instinctively understood as destructive to her soul, did

not occur to her. She knew that she had never violated herself physically, and had never indulged in drink or in the festival antics. She knew that she was blameless of murder or torture. Such innocence, however, did not spare her from remorse over the years wasted without the sacraments, years lost to her in the midst of paganism and persecution. Father Cholenec wrote:

> Every morning, winter and summer, she was in our church at four o'clock, and often she arrived even before the bell which rings every day at that hour. She remained there several hours in succession in prayer, though her tongue played small part in it. Ordinarily, she prayed only with eyes and heart — her eyes suffused with tears, and her heart incessantly giving forth ardent sighs. She was always as if lifted out of herself when she prayed and conversed with Our Lord. Her fervor was no less evident in the confessions which she made every eight days or sometimes oftener. She passed an entire hour in the church weeping and sighing while she prepared herself, and when she began her confession it was always with such loud sobs that she would have given her confessor much difficulty in understanding her, had he not otherwise known her angelical innocence. She thought herself the greatest sinner in the world. It was with such sentiments of humility that she made all her confessions.

Imitating the others, Kateri began a series of physical punishments, using switches to beat her back and shoulders, walking barefoot in the snow, staying awake throughout the night in prayer, and limiting herself to one meal of porridge each day. Such excesses were part of the atonement process of the others. Kateri, who had never indulged in sinful activities as a child or as a young woman, performed them out of recognition of her own failings, and out of love.

The binding power of love became the center of her existence, in fact, rooted in her awareness of the Presence of God. As a mystic, she was acutely aware of the Most Blessed Trinity, the Father, Son, and Holy Spirit, and she understood the simple vocation of each human being on earth — giving praise to the Most High. In this manner, Kateri reflected her patron saint, Catherine of Siena, and the other contemplatives of the past. She was constant in demonstrating her awareness of the Presence of God, using this awareness to spiritualize and perfect even the simplest tasks. There would be other later saints, such as the Little Flower, Saint Thérèse of Lisieux, who would perform their daily routines in the same spirit, thus raising them above the mundane and the common and earning graces for themselves and their contemporaries. How these mortifications were conducted was discussed by Father Cholenec in his account of her life:

> . . . she knew well that God has never so loved mankind as in giving himself to them in the mystery of the Eucharist and on the tree of the Cross. And the saints who have excelled, some in one virtue, others in another, according to the varied attractions of grace, have all merited commendation because of the devotion

they have shown for this double mystery. It may be said that Katharine imitated them perfectly in these two loves and that after having consecrated her heart to Our Lord in the Blessed Sacrament, she sacrificed her body to the Cross, never to be separated from it. She was so eager for the Cross and for suffering that if she had been allowed to act according to the ardor of her desire she would have overwhelmed her body, already infirm and sickly. She sought only to make it suffer in the sight of Jesus crucified. She had for nearly a year and a half with one of her devout companions, several times a week made their shoulders bleed profusely from willow twigs, and they would have continued longer had it not been made a matter of conscience as soon as it was known.

While it is difficult for the modern mind to understand the lengths to which such mystics went in offering God their lives, their talents, and their souls, the love they felt within compelled them to make sacrifices and endure all things. Kateri loved God, gazed upon him with joy. She was being led to the understanding of the true role of the soul in giving praise, in imitating the choirs of angels that surround the throne of God with hymns and chants. Like all mystics before and after her, she was entering the landscape of praise, of worship, of unstinting devotion to the Beloved. Kateri was becoming more alone with the Alone, in the wilderness, in the chapel, even in the company of her fellow mission converts. This was the crux of her life at Sault. She listened to the advice of people like

Anastasia, sought to imitate the tried and true practices of those who repented the past, but she was blameless, innocent, pure as the radiant lily. If she involved herself in excesses, it was not because she sought to distinguish herself in the mission or to court the praise of others; Kateri was a child in the faith, untutored in the more profound areas of mortification and penance. But no one needed to teach her prayer or contemplation, as the Bridegroom had sought her out in the wilderness.

Despite her efforts to remain hidden, Kateri's reputation grew rapidly, and the priests began to understand the significance of Father de Lamberville's letter to them. As a sign of their appreciation of her spirituality, it was announced that Kateri would receive holy Communion at Christmas. She had not yet been allowed to make her first Communion. This was part of the Jesuit approach to conversions, one that extended into all areas of their training. The converts were taught to understand the true essence of the sacraments, and they were allowed to approach them only after demonstrating a solid, unbending adherence to the faith. The fact that the time limit was being waived to some extent for Kateri did not evoke the animosity or envy of her companions. Rather, the chapel was decorated by one and all, a lavish stage for the festivities, as the people sought to honor the events — both the feast itself and Kateri's reception of holy Communion — by incorporating all the traditional symbols of celebration and reverence. Once again pelts, ribbons, feathers, woven tapestries, and other Iroquois ornaments were used to make the chapel a vivid and compelling scene. Certainly the Sault members understood that Kateri was being honored in a singular fashion, and they rejoiced for her.

On the morning of Christmas Day 1677, she approached the altar and made her first holy Communion. She advanced shyly, humbly, quite convinced of her unworthiness to receive Christ. She was one with Christ, united with him, moving toward her ultimate destiny, the final beatific vision in heaven. Nothing else mattered for Kateri Tekakwitha, nothing else had value or significance in her life. Father Cholenec wrote:

> Those who come from the Iroquois are tried out for a long time before they are granted this grace; but it was not so with our Katharine. She had so well prepared herself, and she desired this favor so ardently, that it was granted to her forthwith. She made ready for the great day by extraordinary redoubling of her devotion and afterwards she seemed altogether different, so much was she filled with God and his holy love. One had not to be long in her company to feel it and to be surrounded by it as she was. All her joy was to think upon Our Lord and to converse familiarly with him. She passed almost the entire day, on Sunday and feast days, praying at the foot of the altar, and on working days, she came there to offer up her work.

THE HUNT

Following the Christmas celebrations, which were not only joyous and offered the community the happiness of seeing Kateri receive the holy Eucharist, but filled with the tender moments that always accompany that feast in every land of the world, the Indians departed for the hunting expedition.

This journey into the wilderness, made with the consent and probably the encouragement of the Jesuits, was an extraordinary facet of French mission life among the Native Americans. In accordance with the Jesuit belief in leaving the Native Americans to live their own lives outside the stockade, Christian Native Americans of all Five Nations at Sault maintained their traditions of hunting and gathering in the wilds. Each tribe had a particular destination in mind when they set out, one chosen over the decades for its accessibility and abundance of game. Kateri and the mission Indians packed up their belongings and headed to the Adirondack territory, where the deep forests were cloaked in snow and the air was crisp and clean. Within these deep woods the hunters would search for beaver, ocelot, and other animals, for their pelts and meat. The expedition lasted for four months, and the people usually returned to their homes refreshed and renewed by the solitude, the silence, and the sense of companionship they shared on the trail and in the encampments.

Because this was a time of independence, a looking back to the days of their past, many of the new converts were placed in a position of some spiritual danger. Without the routine of the mission, without the setting, the chapel, and the sacraments, there was a chance that some might relapse into the old ways. For this reason the priests of Sault Mission carefully packed liturgical calendars drawn on bark, as well as prayer schedules and other aids in maintaining an active religious community life. These were carried to the encampment, where they were hung in places of prominence after the cabins of logs and bark skins were erected. It is probable that the remains of old cabins were on the site when they arrived, perhaps rotted and scarred by the winds and the rains, but still evident. The men and women worked together to make them habitable, and then the Woodland Warriors went off into the woods to see what game they could bring back for the hearths.

It was a time of relaxation, even in the cold and the snows. The women had their usual chores, which included treating any animals brought back to the encampment, but the routine was less formal, and the people were able to relax and spend hours in games and in talk. Kateri went to a nearby stream to seek silence and solitude, and she found a small haven formed by overhanging branches there. Carving a cross in the trunk of a tree, she fashioned a chapel of sorts and spent hours in prayer, especially during the time she knew that Mass was being celebrated in the mission chapel. She united herself to this Mass fervently, seeking to accomplish in a truly spiritual sense what she could not manage physically. Back in the camp, she asked constantly for stories about the saints or the chanting of hymns. Most humored her and found their conversations elevated more than usual.

One event took place, however, that would have a very distinct bearing on her life and even on her appearances after death. Kateri was asleep on her mat, or else kneeling in prayer there, when a warrior returned from a day of hunting. Exhausted, unable to spend time finding his own wife's mat in the shadowy confines of the cabin, he stretched out on the floor and fell asleep. In the morning, when his wife awoke and did not find him beside her, she began to look for him. She was shocked to see him asleep close to Kateri. They were not close enough to touch one another, but the man was definitely sleeping in a place he did not belong. The woman, a sincere and good Christian, kept silent about it, but she began to watch her husband and Kateri for other signs of an affair or an involvement. Her alertness paid off when one day she saw her husband building a canoe. Asked by someone if he needed help, he laughed and said Kateri could help him as she was always eager to provide services of charity. That put the seal on the affair as far as the wife was concerned, but she waited until the group had returned to Sault Mission before lodging a complaint.

The converts reached the Sault in time for Palm Sunday, and Kateri was introduced to the liturgical events of Holy Week and the Passion. For someone new to Catholicism, particularly someone not traditionally acquainted with Christianity, the Passion week observances can have a terrible impact. Kateri must have witnessed some sort of liturgical ceremony of the Passion during her time in her village, but what she saw and heard at the Sault Mission reduced her to tears, filled her with a truly profound horror, and prompted her to even greater reparations and self-inflicted penances. Hardships, suffering, and physical pain were not new to the Indians, who recognized in them the way of growing in strength and in spiritual power. Particularly those who had led evil lives in the past resorted to such penances. Kateri, struck by the agonies of Christ, attempted to follow in the same path, to endure, as we have seen, whatever pain she could in order to transform her flesh and to imitate the Savior.

At the same time, however, God had provided yet another torment, in the form of the suspicions of the woman on the hunting expedition. This woman approached Father Cholenec and confided in him. He knew her to be resolute in the faith and sincere, and was quite troubled by the woman's tale. He calmed her, advised her not to spread the story, but he did not react in the way Father de Lamberville had responded to the aunt's gossip of an incestuous relationship. The priest went to Kateri, hoping that she would silence his doubts and his confusion. The priest was clearly concerned by the accusation, and he apparently leaned toward believing it.

Father Cholenec's actions should be judged by the reality of the situation and by the cultural conditioning that he and others had received as a result of being children of their own historical age. To begin with, the presence of Kateri Tekakwitha in the Sault Mission must have disturbed many. She was so amiable, so pious, so resigned to the will of God, so intent upon prayer and sacrifice, that she must have appeared as an alien being, or as something not quite real. Because of human nature, most men and women tend to discount what they see of goodness and holiness, seeking an underlying cause, a slightly distorted view, or a motive. The priests and the other Christian Indians must have wondered silently, if not aloud, how such a paragon of virtue had risen among them. Kateri Tekakwitha was so unlike her Iroquois people, so advanced in spirituality and in saintliness, that she must have been frightening. Father Cholenec, who was charged with the well-being of the entire mission, must have wondered as well about the displays of holiness that Kateri evidenced, despite her humility and her reserve. This does not mean that he doubted Kateri, but he might well have had lingering thoughts about the origin of her actions, the reasons why she was so set apart, so distinguished in matters of the soul.

He went to her with the woman's accusations and was greeted with serene silence. Kateri listened, did not show shock, and did not interrupt his recitation with violent protests. Rather, she calmly announced that nothing of the sort had happened or could happen. She was innocent of all such crimes, and God knew that well enough to provide her with his protection. Father Cholenec, stunned by her acceptance of the accusation and by her resolute announcement that nothing of the sort was possible, let the matter drop. Some of the other converts, however, did hear of it, as the woman accuser was not as discreet as she should have been, and rumors spread about Kateri.

They were not malicious stories, just the sort of dreadful tidbits and tales that humans spread about one another. Certainly the mission people talked about Kateri often enough, and one or two dropped hints that perhaps what they saw on the surface was not exactly the truth of the matter. It was part of the human game of slander, the terrible way in which men and women hurt one another without delivering a physical blow. Because of the mission schedule and the attitude of the local populace, the rumors remained behind closed doors, hidden and never bursting into the public humiliations that Kateri had suffered in the past. If they looked at her with wonder, they said nothing and made no effort to hinder her spiritual growth.

On Palm Sunday, when Kateri was allowed to receive holy

Communion for the second time, the entire community was edified by the change that came over her during her union with Christ. That afternoon she was also inducted into the Brotherhood of the Holy Family, a rare honor. If the woman with the suspicions felt irritation or anger over the honor, she said and did nothing. Kateri became one of the select group of Christians at the mission, despite her young age and her lowly status as a new convert. The entire community greeted this advance with the usual demonstration of delight and rejoicing.

Perhaps when confronted by the accusation, or during the following hours, Kateri began to understand that her death was fast approaching. She would have embraced such a premonition with indescribable joy, as she was about to be set free from the world. Her reputation and her good name no longer mattered, and she rejoiced in being reviled for something that she did not do. Christ, the Sinless, had been slain as a common criminal by men of evil ambitions. The sort of mental suffering she endured was mild compared to his pains, and she put all thought of her reputation aside. The heavenly Father would make her known in his time, and her name would be glorified when he chose to confound her enemies and to edify the innocent.

CHAPTER SEVEN

SAINT KATERI'S LAST DAYS

. . . her soul acquired new strength in proportion as her body decayed. The nearer she approached the end of her days, the more clearly she shone forth in all those virtues which she had practiced with so much edification.

Father Pierre Cholenec, S.J.

Returning from the hunt, Kateri resolved never to attend another such expedition. When the group set out the next year, she refused and explained to the priests that the excursions provided physical benefits but brought cruel sufferings to her soul by denying her the sacraments and the presence of Christ upon the altar.

An accident that took place while she was out gathering wood and felling trees convinced Kateri that she was in God's hands alone. A large tree limb crashed to the ground, striking her on the head. Unconscious for a time, she was revived by her companion and urged to return to the mission. Kateri only smiled and thanked God for saving her life. Her frail health had always been a challenge, from surviving smallpox and living with its damage to her eyesight, to enduring the abuse of her companions in the village. For Kateri, the life eternal became paramount to her, and she was concerned solely with perfecting herself in preparation for it and with making herself worthy. But she had also found a haven, a place of refuge at the Sault Mission, and in that haven she was able to perfect the virtues and find the kind of spiritual support and friendship that she had always wanted. The two friends who played a role in Kateri's life at the Sault Mission were Anastasia and Marie Theresa Tegaigenta.

Anastasia, the older woman who was matriarch of the family Kateri lived with, was much revered by the Christian Indians. She was among the very first of the Iroquois to be converted and baptized, and she became one of the leading Christians in the mission. She was especially adept at instructing others in the faith.

There began an immediate friendship between the women, and Anastasia taught Kateri much about the village and her duties, as well as assisting the Jesuits in guiding Kateri's catechetical development. Father Chauchetière described their friendship:

> She [Kateri] was never idle for a moment, whether she was in the lodge, in the fields, or in the forest. One saw her, rosary in hand, with her dear instructress, going and coming, carrying her share of the wood. The most menial occupations were raised by the fervor and spirit

with which Katharine did them. She never separated from Anastasia because she learned more when the two went together for wood than at any other time. Her manner of action made Anastasia say that Katharine never lost sight of God.

Anastasia's method in instructing Katharine was to ask her what she had done in her country during the time that they had been separated from each other. She sounded Katharine on the attachment which she might have for the glass beads which she wore around her neck and in her hair. She asked her if she did not wish to marry, as she was already of marriageable age. Katharine completely bared her conscience concerning things, telling her she had always lived according to the customs she had observed among the Iroquois, always belittling herself and confessing her ignorance. When Anastasia spoke to her of slander which she must avoid, Katharine said she did not know what slander was. One must not be astonished that she did not know its meaning, either in theory or practice, since no one had ever heard her speak ill of any person, not even of those who calumniated her.

Anastasia was a true friend to Kateri all her days. In the brief years remaining to Kateri, however, Anastasia was rapidly eclipsed in knowledge of the faith and also in fervor by her young friend. This was not a competition, of course, between Kateri and Anastasia, but the priests were able to see Kateri's remarkable progress in the Catholic faith. And they had as the grounds for comparison the dedication and zeal of Anastasia.

Kateri's second friend was a woman born as Tegaigenta to the Oneida nation. She had endured a very difficult life in the wilderness and had become a Christian and been baptized Marie Theresa. She had lapsed at times into the old ways, especially showing a sad tendency toward drunkenness. In 1675, she came finally to La Prairie Mission with her husband, and from there they went on a winter hunt. Her nephew came with them, and they joined another group of Iroquois, consisting of four men, four women, and three children, who were on their way to a campsite normally erected along the Ottawa River. The group looked forward to pleasant days and good hunting.

Several miles into the wilderness, however, they became caught in a terrible blizzard, with winds and storms raging over their heads. The snow fell everywhere, burying the plants and sending the game into hiding. The hunters in the group were able to kill only one animal, which they cooked and ate to keep up their strength. The meat did not last, of course, and within days they were all starving again, with no signs of a change in the weather and little chance of survival.

The women stewed the skins that they carried in their packs, making a soup from any bits of flesh or fat still on them, to feed their companions. While the hunters wandered about in the storm, the women gathered tree bark and soaked that as well, trying to make it edible. Others crawled around on the ground looking for tubers, grass, and other plants. Nothing could be provided for the cooking pots, and even in shelters the fires went out and the chill of the wind and snow ate into their weakened bodies.

Marie Theresa's husband fell ill as a result, and as she stayed to care for him, two hunters went on ahead. One returned from this venture alone, and the others dared not look at him because he appeared well fed and rested. It was obvious to one and all that the warrior had slain his companion and roasted his flesh in order to stave off his own starvation.

Marie Theresa's husband did not recover, and when the group decided to retrace their steps in hopes of reaching the mission before their hunger killed them, the warrior who had returned alone insisted that she abandon her husband and come with them. She refused. Her nephew, who was also ill, stayed with her. She nursed her husband until he died a few days later, and she mourned him and buried his corpse so that the scavenging birds and wild animals would not devour his flesh. Then, carrying her sick nephew on her back, she trudged along the trail left by the group and caught up with them. A new round of horrors began then, as the warriors intended to murder one of the women and her two children, to eat them and survive. Knowing that Marie Theresa was a Christian, they asked her opinion of the deed, filling her with revulsion and terror. Knowing that if she tried to stop them the men would slay her and her nephew, she kept silent. Inwardly, however, she was sick with grief and begged God's forgiveness for her cowardice and her refusal to risk all by stopping them. The woman and her children died at the hands of the warriors, and their bodies were eaten. Marie Theresa was hysterical by this time, begging God's forgiveness over and over and promising to change her life if she survived this terrible ordeal.

By the time the band arrived at La Prairie, there were only a few of them left, and the survivors bore the marks — physical and spiritual — of their ordeal.

Maria Theresa wasted no time keeping her promise. She confessed her sins to the startled and shocked priest, and she made good on her word, taking on the Christian way of life with a fierce steadfastness that she never lost.

She moved with the mission to Sault in 1676 and continued her life there, meeting Kateri Tekakwitha in the spring of 1678. The young Mohawk maiden asked Marie Theresa which side she should use in the chapel, adding that she felt that she did not have a right to enter, being sinful and unworthy of such a distinct honor. The words struck Marie Theresa in her heart, and she wept and confided the sordid tale of her conversion, the experiences of the hunt, and her efforts to live a life of atonement. Kateri, taken aback by the horrors the woman had endured and by her honesty and sincere desire to live a virtuous life, opened up her own heart, and in time the two women became close friends. Anastasia was elderly and now unable to work in the fields or the forests. Although she remained close to Kateri, both knew that she needed a companion closer to her own age. Kateri and Marie Theresa thus began to do their daily chores together, go to chapel together, and encourage one another to heights of perfection.

The relationship, of course, was quite unequal in a spiritual sense, as Marie Theresa probably had no idea of the depths of Kateri's holiness or the mystical form it had assumed. She was a woman who had experienced the world, had married, had been a drunk, and had taken part in a grisly episode on the wilderness trail. As a result, the faith was a haven for her, and she lived to atone for her own evils and the evils of her people. Kateri, who appeared to Marie Theresa to have never sinned — a fact that Marie Theresa reported later by stating that the only fault Kateri could manage to call down upon herself was working in the fields on the Sabbath — walked the rare and beautiful landscape of a soul in tune with the vibrancies of Divine Love. They blended, however, sometimes falling into the error of excesses in penance, sometimes trying to assume too many self-inflicted punishments, but always seeking God in their lives and existing within the Presence even in the mundane routines of their mission world.

MONTRÉAL

Sometime after meeting Marie Theresa, Kateri was invited in some fashion to visit Ville-Marie, the city of Montréal, where she discovered aspects of the spiritual life that had been instinctive in her and yet never visibly demonstrated. She returned with a new goal, a new horizon opening before her, the last stage in her spiritual growth and the one that would transport her into the Divine Embrace forever.

Montréal was originally a Huron settlement called Hocelaga, and was visited by Jacques Cartier in 1535. This intrepid explorer was welcomed by over one thousand Hurons on the slopes of Mount Royal, and there he made friends with the Huron nation and its honorable traditions and lore. Eventually, the Hurons abandoned the site, moving to Place Royale on the Saint Lawrence River, a settlement founded by Samuel de Champlain. Hocelaga ceased to exist, reverting to its natural wild and beautiful state until May 6, 1642, when another Frenchman, Paul de Chomedey — called in accounts the Sieur de Maisonnueve — arrived and started a colonial town there. He called his settlement Ville-Marie, the "Town of Mary," and he erected several residences and a chapel, working toward the construction of a hospital and a school as well. The site was given a civic charter by King Louis XIV in 1644 and was well on its way to becoming the seat of New France. Chomedey was honored by being appointed the first governor of the town and probably the immediate region.

Encouraged by this development, two saintly women arrived in Ville-Marie to found a hospital, the famed Hôtel-Dieu, and the local schools. The white children were educated in Ville-Marie, and a school was established for Native Americans at the Mission of La Montagne. Kateri, probably in the company of a priest and other converts, discovered the work of the women who had come to dedicate their lives to Christ and to their fellow human beings, and the sight of them sent her soul soaring.

She belonged in a religious convent, as a cloister with its routines and carefully structured spiritual exercises would have provided her with a stable framework for her mystical experiences. Native American vocations, however, were unheard of, probably never even contemplated, especially by the Europeans. They would have been hard-pressed to consider any Indian maiden intellectually or spiritually inclined enough to assume such a position of leadership and authority. That racial barrier, a product of the times, did not fall for a considerable length of time.

Kateri returned to the mission and spoke of the religious life to Marie Theresa. Father Chauchetière wrote:

> . . . each day Katharine and Therese [sic] performed some act of devotion which was proper and suitable for their aim. Marie Therese . . . thought it would be better if there were a third, or if they had some other Christian girl with them from whom they could learn all they wished to know. She added that she knew one named Marie Skarichions, who had lived for a long time at Québec and at the Mission of Our Lady of Lorette, conducted on the same plan as the Mission of the Sault. When Katharine agreed with her companion's suggestion, the three assembled at the foot of the cross, which was planted on the riverside. There the elder companion spoke first, expressed her desire to join them, and proposed that they adopt the rule of life of the Religious she had seen. . . . Accordingly, they chose as their home an island called Heron Island. All this was made part of their deliberations, because they had but the concept of the basic foundations of religious life. Katharine thanked the speaker with tears of joy in her eyes, and begged her to keep nothing from them which would make them more pleasing to God. Although the others had persisted in their resolution to give themselves entirely to God and never to marry, none of them had profited as much as Katharine in

perseveringly following the rule of life which her confessor had given her.

THE VOW

In due course, one of the women went to Father Frémin to discuss their idea of the religious life in isolation and to seek his counsel, especially as they did not wish to undertake anything that was not appropriate or that might endanger their spiritual well-being. The priest felt compelled to discourage their plans. He told them that they were all too young, that Heron Island was too remote and removed from proper oversight of the mission, and above all that its location so close to Montréal would mean that visitors, especially men, would be arriving on the island constantly, more so once word spread of the sudden appearance of a religious camp filled with young Native girls.

There was certainly a European prejudice at work, a difficulty comprehending the spiritual aspirations for the consecrated life as valid in the souls of the Native Americans. Today many members of the various Indian nations have assumed not only religious roles but appointments as prelates throughout the nation. In Kateri's time, however, the supposed disability of living in the wilderness was still prevailing in the minds of the whites, including the missionaries. However, a type of religious organization did take root after Kateri's death, with Marie Theresa leading the devout maidens who wanted to live by the example of the Lily of the Mohawks.

Nevertheless, Father Frémin spoke to Kateri about her

own spiritual destiny and what he saw was her definite yearning for a specific state of life.

Anastasia urged Kateri to accept a warrior as a husband. Father Frémin was aware that there was a natural cultural inclination toward marriage in the village. The Christian Indians were acting out of concern for her and because the custom of marriage was so ingrained in the Native American heritage. It was fit and just for a woman to want a husband and children, to desire to become a matron leader and to exercise her authority within the community. Certainly the Iroquois had honored their matrons over the centuries, entrusting them with legal and political rights that were quite sophisticated, especially when compared with the lot of most European women.

Kateri's relative began nagging her, complaining that eventually she would have to have a husband to provide for her, hinting that in time they would not be so willing to make room for her in their cabin. The "sister" told Kateri to think about it, convinced as Kateri's aunts had been in the village that the woman would come to her senses and accept the inevitable choice. Kateri went to Father Cholenec, who felt perhaps that marriage would safeguard her, yet understood that her soul was destined for a different role. He assured her that she was quite free to choose a virginal existence, and if she did, the mission would always come to her aid. Father Cholenec reported that he told her that while he supported her plans not to marry, he urged her to take three days to contemplate it and pray on it.

Once she heard those words, Kateri's entire appearance changed. She became radiant and calm, and the peace that had entered her soul in that instant radiated outward. He said that she had "entered veritably into the joy of the Lord." That demonstration, that visible display of union, made the missionary even more ardent in protecting her unusual status. Kateri went away, but returned after a mere quarter of an hour. Father Cholenec reported their conversation. "'It is settled,' said she, as she came near me; 'it is not a question for deliberation; my part has long since been taken. No my Father, I can have no other spouse but Jesus Christ.' I thought that it would be wrong for me any longer to oppose a resolution which seemed to me inspired by the Holy Spirit, and therefore exhorted her to perseverance, assuring her that I would take her part against those who wished henceforth to disturb her on that subject." She later declared, "I am no longer my own. I have given myself entirely to Jesus Christ."

When Anastasia came a few days later to complain that Kateri had refused them all, he scolded her and explained that some souls were chosen to perform distinct and unusual acts for the love of God. Confronted with another point of view, Anastasia accepted the priest's words and returned to the cabin to silence the relatives forever. If they clung to their Iroquois traditions inwardly, they said nothing more to Kateri.

Kateri, meanwhile, was eager to make formal the private pledge she had taken of perpetual virginity. Father Cholenec recorded the event in his 1715 letter to Father Le Blanc:

> For this great event she chose the day on which we celebrate the festival of the Annunciation of the Most Holy Virgin. The next moment after she had received Our Lord in holy Communion, she pronounced with

admirable fervor the vow she had made of perpetual virginity. She then addressed the Holy Virgin, for whom she had a most tender devotion, praying her to present to her Son the oblation of herself which she had just made; after which she passed some hours at the foot of the altar in holy meditation and in perfect union with God.

Father Cholenec noted further that from that time until her death, Kateri seemed to be entirely divorced from this world. She had turned her attentions exclusively to the anticipation of heaven. That eternal destiny was her goal, and everything else, every earthly attachment, had ceased to have any influence on her. Father Chauchetière wrote of the next months that passed:

Katharine entered with renewed fervor into the preparations for the feasts of Saint Francis Xavier, patron of the Sault, and for Christmas, which was drawing near. This would be the second Christmas she had spent at the Sault, for it was a year and a half since she had come from her own country. She would have cut her hair if the fear of seeming too virtuous had not overwhelmed her, and so she contented herself with wearing it like the other modest young girls of the village. Father Frémin had given her a rule of life different from that of the others. He instructed her to be retiring, above all; that in summer, when the canoes of the Ottawas would come, she must stay in her cabin and not go to the river bank with the others to see their

arrival. . . . She renounced all the red clothing and ornaments of the savages and only wore a new and simple
blue dress on the days when she received holy Communion. Though she brought with her simple clothing a
perfect heart which God alone could see, she could not
conceal her devotion so that her companion did not but
notice it in moments of their greatest fervor together.

Father Cholenec, however, also noted that her body was
not able to endure the weight of her austerities and what he
declared was "the constant effort of her spirit to maintain itself
in the presence of God." Thus by the time the winter snows
covered the earth in late 1679, Kateri was failing in health. She
had always been frail, of course, but her pain had been growing
and she was increasingly exhausted. She remained in her cabin,
unable to attend the services in the chapel and yet filled with
calm and joy. The Jesuit wrote that there took place in her a
powerful transformation:

> . . . her soul acquired new strength in proportion as her
> body decayed. The nearer she approached the end of
> her days, the more clearly she shone forth in all those
> virtues which she had practiced with so much edifica-
> tion. . . . She had a most tender love for God. Her only
> pleasure seemed to be to keep herself in contemplation
> in his presence, to meditate on his majesty and mercy,
> to sing his praises, and continually to desire new ways
> of pleasing him. It was principally to prevent distrac-
> tion from other thoughts that she so often withdrew

into solitude. Anastasia and Theresa were the only two Christians with whom she wished much to associate because they talked most of God, and their conversation breathed nothing but divine love.

Father Cholenec took to visiting her in the cabin, bringing holy pictures that she would hold and study. He also brought writings from the Old and New Testaments, inscribed on birch bark. Kateri spent long hours with these pictures and writings, content to remain in her confined area and yet managing somehow to influence life around her at the same time. The Indians began to visit her as well, asking for her counsel and guidance. They knew that the Lily of the Mohawks was about to leave Sault Mission. According to Father Chauchetière:

> When she could go out, it was her pleasure to be in the church part of the day, kneeling, or resting on the benches when she could not support herself. If she remained in the cabin alone, as frequently happens to the sick among people who are occupied in the fields, she communed with God. Truly, on such occasions she never lost sight of him, whether in meditating or saying her Rosary. When the priest who had care of the sick visited her, she thought more of her soul than of her body and her illness.

Intense physical suffering began soon after her initial collapse. She was unable to move, remaining still on her pallet but demonstrating her serene and gentle outlook. Father Cholenec described her suffering and her serenity:

> Her patience was the test in every trial. In the midst of her continual infirmities she always preserved a peace and serenity of spirit which charmed us. She never forgot herself either to utter a complaint or give the slightest sign of impatience. During the last two months of her life her sufferings were extraordinary. She was obliged to remain night and day in the same position. The very least movement caused her the most intense pain, But when these pains were at their worst, she seemed most content, esteeming herself happy, as she herself said, to live and to die on the cross, uniting her sufferings to those of the Savior.

THE FINAL HOURS

Her condition worsened steadily, and with the approach of Holy Week everyone in Sault Mission recognized the signs of her coming death. The priests decided to bring her viaticum, the Communion offered to the sick and the dying. This was an unusual decision, as the priests normally did not carry the Blessed Sacrament out of the chapel in those times. In the early mission stages it was considered too dangerous to expose the Host to the rough and tumble atmosphere of the cabins and the general camps. In Kateri's state, however, it was deemed a necessity. She could not be brought to the chapel on a stretcher, as it was feared that she would not make the short trip alive, and no one wanted to deny her the Blessed Sacrament. After consulting with the elders of the mission, the priests informed her that they would bring Communion to her in her bed.

Delighted that such a blessing was going to be given to her, Kateri confided in Marie Theresa that she had nothing to wear for the occasion. Although she had made clothing, even elaborate moccasins for everyone else, she had nothing but a ragged shift for her own body. Marie Theresa brought a fine outfit for her to wear, and a radiant Kateri awaited the priests who came in a procession with the Blessed Host.

Following her reception of the holy Eucharist, Kateri was visited by all her mission companions. The Brotherhood of the Holy Family remained ever at her side, coming two by two to keep vigil and to see to her comfort. During one of their hours of care, a young woman who had great devotion to Kateri went into the forest to perform harsh physical penances in order to insure an easy death for the Lily of the Mohawks. Kateri knew that she had set out to do this and sent for her. When the startled young woman appeared, Kateri urged her to practice moderation and to be assured that after her death she would pray for her and be a guardian always. The girl was reduced to tears and knelt beside Kateri, remaining at her side.

Her condition worsened steadily, and the others watched as her skin darkened and her body contorted in pain. Father Cholenec, ever watchful, informed her then that he would bring Extreme Unction, the last rites that would put the seal of her faith on her dying body. Kateri told him not to hurry, as she would be able to receive it the next day. She knew the hour of her death and waited with calm for the approaching last embrace. When the priests returned the next day, Kateri was still alive, watching them with half-blind eyes, small, delicate, and wrapped in her last mortal agonies.

On April 17, 1680, at the age of twenty-four, Kateri Tekakwitha left behind all the landscapes of this world. Father Chauchetière wrote a detailed account of her last moments:

> Finally, having difficulty in speaking and not being able to raise her voice, and seeing her comrade [Theresa] bathed in tears, she bade her a last farewell. "I am leaving you," said Katharine. "I am about to die. Always remember what we have done together since we knew each other; if you change I will accuse you before the tribunal of God. Take courage, despise the discourse of those who have no faith, when they wish to persuade you to marry; listen only to the priests. If you cannot serve God here go to the Lorette Mission. Never give up mortification. I will love you in heaven. I will pray for you, I will assist you."

> The priest, who was kneeling near to say the last prayers for the dying, heard a little of what Katharine said. He kept his eyes fixed on her face to observe what was happening and even encouraged her friends. Katharine's face was turned toward heaven. Her companion embraced her with one hand, supporting her chin with the other, and listening with attention to the last words of the dying Katharine.

> This blessed daughter, in saying to her companion, "I

will love you in heaven," lost her voice for a time when phlegm began to choke her. For a long time her eyes had been closed to created things; now she could not speak, but to the very last breath she could hear well.

It was remarked several times that when some act was suggested to her, she took new strength, but that when she was exhorted to the love of God the expression of her face seemed to change. Everyone wished to share in the devotion that her dying countenance inspired. It appeared more like the face of one in contemplation than the face of one dying. Thus she remained until her last breath. Her respiration diminished constantly from about nine o'clock until ten and finally became barely perceptible, though her expression remained unchanged. One of the priests, kneeling at her right side, noticed only a slight contraction of the nerve at the right side of her mouth, and so she died as if she were falling asleep. For some time no one was sure she was dead.

Her last known words were: "Jesus, I love you."

The Indians crowded into the cabin to be present at her death, and they wept and mourned their loss. For more than an hour the cabin was filled with weeping and exhortations that they should always follow her example.

Father Cholenec and the others soon discovered the first sign of Kateri in her unearthly vocation. The body of Kateri had been laid out on a pallet, but it was no longer the frail, dark, and scarred young woman who had just expired. Her skin had lightened, becoming radiant and white, and the scars vanished from her face, showing the beautiful contours and the lovely angles of her heritage. The people gasped, for before them lay an exquisite creature restored. Father Cholenec wrote:

> Due to smallpox, Katharine's face had been disfigured since the age of four, and her infirmities and mortifications had contributed to disfigure her even more, but this face, so marked and swarthy, suddenly changed about a quarter of an hour after her death, and became in a moment so beautiful and so white that I observed it immediately (for I was praying beside her) and cried out, so great was my astonishment. I had them call the Father who was working in the repository for Holy Thursday. He came, as did the Indians, on hearing of this wonder, which we were able to contemplate until her burial. I admit openly that the first thought that came to me was that Katharine at that moment might have entered into heaven, reflecting in her chaste body a small ray of the glory of which her soul had taken possession.

At that point, two Frenchmen who were well acquainted with the Lily of the Mohawks chanced by and entered the cabin. They took one look at the body and asked what lovely maiden slept there, surrounded by the people. Father Cholenec explained that it was Kateri, who had died just an hour before, and the two men knelt beside her and wept. They were stunned by the changes, which they knew demonstrated Kateri's true beauty in the eyes of God. They volunteered to make an elaborate coffin for her burial and set out to take down the trees and begin carving the box that would hold her remains.

PART THREE

THE LEGACY OF
SAINT KATERI

All her joy was to think upon Our Lord and to converse familiarly with Him. She passed almost the entire day, on Sundays and feast days, praying at the foot of the altar, and on working days she often came there to offer up her work. . . .

Father Pierre Cholenec, S.J.

CHAPTER EIGHT

THE HOLINESS OF SAINT KATERI

In her great and glorious title of virgin, however, Katharine was
more blessed than others and attained a higher place, not only
among the Indians of the Sault, but also among all those in
Northern France who embraced the faith. . . .

Father Claude Chauchetière, S.J.

The writings of Fathers Jacques de Lamberville, Pierre Cholenec, and Claude Chauchetière were vital in preserving our awareness of Saint Kateri, and are especially significant for their important role in arguing for her sanctity and spiritual legacy. As was noted in the Introduction, the French Jesuits, learned and seasoned missionary priests, stood in wonder of the Indian maiden whom they had known only briefly, but who was the model par excellence in their minds, not only for Native American Catholics but for Catholics anywhere.

Significantly, the French priests were edified by the faith of the Native Americans who had come into the Church, even as they held up Kateri as the greatest exemplar of the faith from among those they served. Father Cholenec wrote:

> As we have remarked before, the Mission of the Sault was at that time very fervent under the guidance of its holy missionaries. It was a new church, possessed of extraordinary graces, and the holiness which prevailed there was worthy of the early Church. The Iroquois had become strongly attached to the Church, and these ardent and brave neophytes had conceived such sorrow and shame for the sins of their past lives that even though these had been effaced by baptism, they still performed great penances for them. . . .

> They lived in great innocence, union, and charity, especially as regards the poor and sick, and did not content themselves in working for their own salvation, but were also zealous for their compatriots who came to the Sault, either to visit or live with them. . . .

> Such great and beautiful actions deserve to be known and praised by all, but those who performed them had as much humility as fervor, and knew how to hide their mortification so well, that except for the missionaries nearby, no one knew of them.

The esteem for Kateri was notable virtually from the time that Father de Lamberville first encountered her in her cabin. He wrote of the great impression she had made upon him at that meeting, and that he was firmly convinced from that early meeting that this young Indian maiden was destined for great things in the spiritual realm. His expectations and those of the fellow Jesuits were more than exceeded by Kateri in the years after her baptism. She developed swiftly in the virtues as was recorded especially by Fathers Cholenec and Chauchetière in their biographies.

The account of Kateri's life by Father Chauchetière was written in 1685, five years after Kateri's death. It was clearly crafted not only to highlight her life but to build a powerful case, an argument, for her holiness and the impact she had on those around her, including the priests who served at the Sault Mission. The French Jesuit went to great efforts to document Kateri's spirituality, her devotion to the Eucharist, and her reputation for holiness, which had spread across the whole of French Canada. His view was shared by Father de Lamberville and Father Cholenec. To read their description of Kateri and their assessment of her holiness is to encounter experienced priests and spiritual leaders who readily recognized the universal traits of sanctity.

For the Church, the certification of the perfection of the virtues to a heroic degree is one of the most crucial elements in the final determination of a person's status as a saint. According to her biographers, Kateri manifested this heroic perfection of the virtues, including the theological virtues and the cardinal virtues. Father Cholenec, for example, wrote that he would not even try to recount all her virtues because the task would be too extensive. He did, however, enumerate several, including her faith, hope, love of God, love of neighbor, prudence, religion, devotion, penance, chastity, and obedience. Father Chauchetière taught that charity is the queen of virtues, enriching all the others and proving the source of holiness, and he cited the example of Saint Paul's desire to love God with one's entire heart, the safest and surest road to holiness and perfection. He wrote:

> Keeping this in mind, it is not difficult to believe that Katharine became perfect in so short a time, considering the ardor of her love for God. She loved him so much that her only joy was to think of him and to offer him all her thoughts, words, and actions. . . . It has been told of several saints, that at times their hearts were so inflamed with divine love, that in spite of the efforts they took to hide this sacred fire, which consumed them from within, they were unable to prevent the escape of some of its sparks. Such was Katharine's love. This young girl, although only an untutored Indian, was so filled with the spirit of God, and tasted such sweetness in its possession, that her entire exterior gave testimony of it; her eyes, her gestures, her words, were filled with divine love at such moments. If one were with her, it did not take long to be touched by it, and to become warmed with this heavenly fire.

Father Chauchetière saw this love for God as the basis for Kateri's great religious fervor, her love for the Eucharist and the Blessed Virgin Mary, and her prayer life.

Father Cholenec described her commitment to be a saint:

Katharine was not satisfied with an ordinary life; driven by this insatiable desire for good and by her extreme fervor to undertake and accomplish much, she began by embracing what was most perfect. She took for her principal, or rather for her only maxim, to search in all things for what would be most pleasing to God, not to reserve anything from him and to make it a rule to give him everything that depended on her, without any respect for creatures and without any return for herself. So holy a maxim had as its foundation the exalted idea that she was made to the likeness of God, and the extreme gratefulness she felt and retained during her entire life for the great grace God had bestowed on her in choosing her among so many others whom he left in the darkness, to see the Light. . . .

Father Cholenec compared her special love of the mission church to other Christians of his experience who were less than zealous in their prayer life or who went to the church to make a pretend show of their fidelity. She managed always to do the tasks that had been appointed her in the community, but she also chose not to waste her time in what she saw as distractions from her singular focus on God. This was partly why she spent so much of her brief life in contemplative prayer in the church and why she sought to turn every form of labor into a prayerful act.

Kateri found God everywhere, wrote Father Cholenec,

whether she was in a church, in the forest, in the fields, or in her cabin. She walked always with a rosary in her hand so as not to allow her time going about the camp to be spent outside of some form of prayer. When the frequently severe winters struck the mission and all but shut down the daily routine, Kateri did not engage in evenings filled with gossip and chatter. The members of the community knew that she would be found in only one place: the church, passing the night in prayer before the Blessed Sacrament.

Kateri was also ardent in her embrace of the Sacrament of Reconciliation. She faithfully ended each week with a careful examination of conscience, a full accounting of her actions and thoughts. She then gave a confession every Saturday night to one of the priests and received both absolution and spiritual counsel. Her examen (or examination of conscience) was usually conducted in seclusion, and she often went into the woods for this purpose. The priests never divulged what she confessed, but Father Cholenec referred in his writings to Kateri's "angelic innocence."

Having prepared her soul through the Sacrament of Reconciliation, Kateri was able always to demonstrate an abiding love of the Eucharist. Father Cholenec wrote of the way this was related to her general commitment to the Christian faith:

> The same fervor was especially evident every time she received holy Communion. Those who come from the Iroquois are tried out for a long time before they are granted this grace; but it was not so with our Katharine. . . . One had not to be long in her company to

feel it and to be surrounded by it as she was. All her joy was to think upon Our Lord and to converse familiarly with him. She passed almost the entire day, on Sundays and feast days, praying at the foot of the altar, and on working days she often came there to offer up her work . . . she knew well that God has never so loved mankind as in giving himself to them in the mystery of the Eucharist and on the tree of the Cross. And the saints who have excelled, some in one virtue, others in another according to the varied attractions of grace, have all merited commendation because of the devotion they have shown for this double mystery.

Father Chauchetière was able to expand further on her demeanor before the Blessed Sacrament. He wrote that she entered the mission church, took holy water — to remind herself especially of her baptism and her resolve to live as a devout Christian — and then knelt in a corner of the church so as to avoid distracting or interrupting any others there. She then typically covered her head with her blanket and made an Act of Faith in the Real Presence in the Blessed Sacrament. She also then made an interior act of contrition or some self-reflection out of humility. She prayed for her own people, her friends, and her relatives, and concluded by saying a Rosary. Typically, she visited the church five times a day, and it was said that if one needed to find her, look first in the church.

Likewise, she had a devotion to the Blessed Mother. She had great love of her own mother, and she had from the very time of her arrival at the Sault Mission been careful to mark the feast days of the Virgin Mary and looked to her especially as a model in her own commitment to chastity. Father Chauchet- ière observed:

> "The virginity that Katharine always loved, that she preserved at the cost of her bodily life, was the reason of her frequent recourse to the Blessed Virgin; for she regarded her life as a model to be imitated as much as possible. This desire led her to make the procession . . . around the fields in the snow, saying the Rosary many times. She was never without her rosary. She had learned by heart the Litany of the Blessed Virgin and never failed to say it in private after the night prayers were said together in the cabin."

The recitation of the Rosary in the snow, of course, was only one of Kateri's many personal mortifications and aus- terities. Her penances were described by the Jesuits, who un- derstood that the actions — at times performed to excessive degrees — were in emulation of the sufferings of the saints and out of a desire to share in the Cross.

Encouraged by Marie Theresa, who had so much to repent, Kateri undertook heavy physical penances, including beatings, branding herself, wearing an iron waist chain, kneeling in the snow, walking barefoot in the dead of winter, and even trying to sleep on thorns. She continued the practices, including kneel- ing in the snow and walking barefoot in the dead of winter. The physical exertions and punishments quickly took their toll on her. Kateri became quite ill, so alarming Marie Theresa that her companion in these moritifcations went to Father Cholenec to explain what they had been doing. He discouraged any type of excess and made them promise to use discretion, even as he recognized the traditions of the Native Americans and the piety that compelled Kateri to undertake extreme measures of sacrifice for God. Kateri began to exercise greater prudence and soon was able to continue her normal routines. Equally, the sure and swift obedience that she displayed when ordered to ease her personal austerities was taken by the priests as a sign of her spiritual docility and her desire not to err in her labors to perfect the virtues.

The members of the community, of course, were fully aware of Kateri's many spiritual gifts, and also her strength of character in facing adversity. Her conversion to the Church had imposed on her severe treatment by her Mohawk family and clan, and she had borne the suffering with great fortitude. It should not have been a surprise, then, that when she declared her unwillingness to marry in order to give herself to Christ, she remained firm in her commitment. Nevertheless, her small circle of friends at Sault took it upon themselves to encourage and nudge her gently to consider marriage. As we have seen, the chief figure in this was the loving and certainly well-meaning Anastasia. Father Cholenec documented the last great effort by Anastasia to bring Kateri around to the idea of marriage. This exchange led not only to Kateri's firm resolve not to wed but to her taking the vow of perpetual virginity and proposing the formation of a small religious community.

As we've seen, Kateri had been greatly impressed by the women religious she had met at Ville-Marie. Whatever preparations she made internally, she finally approached Father Cholenec and asked him to allow her to make a vow of perpetual virginity and chastity. She believed that the purity of thought and actions performed by all true Christians, especially those who had pledged themselves as spouses of Christ, had enormous appeal to God, and she wanted to accomplish all that she could while she still had time.

Father Cholenec was astounded. Such a vow was unprecedented in the missions, especially among the Native Americans, whose traditions ran contrary to such ideals. The missionary understood, of course, that it was shocking to the Native Americans that Kateri had held herself aloof from the customary physical activities of the villages, and had guarded her virginity and her soul always. Seeing the nuns in Ville-Marie had confirmed what grace and her instincts had taught her over the years, and she understood now that she wanted to pledge herself to Christ for the brief period of time that she had left. This union, this marriage in the spirit, would only be a foretaste of what she would experience when her life on earth ended. She wanted to be the spouse of the Divine Bridegroom, and she knew that it was a tradition in the Church that pious women were able to take such a pledge upon themselves. Father Cholenec still saw this as truly unparalleled:

> The thing was so unusual, however, and appeared so incompatible with the life of the Indians, that I thought it best not to precipitate matters, so as to give her plenty of time to weigh a matter of such consequence. I tried her, therefore, for some time, and after

I had noted the great progress she made in every kind of virtue, and above all with the profusion God communed with his servant, it seemed to me that Katharine's design could come from no other source than from him. Thereupon, I at least gave her permission to carry it out. It would be hard to put in words the joy she felt and the fervor with which she prepared for so great an act. But when this day, so longed for, the happiest and most beautiful of her life, at last arrived, she made one more effort to offer her sacrifice to the Lord with all the devotion and ardor she could command.

On the feast of the Annunciation, when the Virgin Mother of God asked the Angel of the Lord how she could become a mother, not having known a man, Kateri Tekakwitha, a daughter of the American wilderness, consecrated her virginity, her purity, and her very soul to Christ. She made this vow on March 25, 1679. In his recounting of her virtues, Father Cholenec gave a fitting testimony of her chastity: "This is the most beautiful flower in all her crown. . . . Men, God, and her conscience have testified to the truth that Katharine never committed a single sin of the flesh. When they questioned her at baptism, when they questioned her at her death, she replied in a firm tone that she did not fear to be damned for this sin. God wished her to appear after her death to two people who were in doubt of what they should think concerning her and her purity."

In looking back on the occasion and on the important spiritual step taken by Kateri, Father Cholenec stated that she had never been untrained in virtue. She had been God's servant since the first inklings of faith had made their way into her soul unbidden, even in the uproar and the barbarism of Mohawk village life. The priests and her fellow Christians taught her the niceties, the rituals, and the forms of Christianity, but the Holy Spirit instructed her in the essence, in the profound realities of such beliefs.

Father Chauchetière was likewise edified by Kateri's commitment to virginity. He wrote:

> In her great and glorious title of virgin, however, Katharine was more blessed than others and attained a higher place, not only among the Indians of the Sault, but also among all those in Northern France who embraced the faith; for because she was the first in the new world, who by a special inspiration of the Holy Ghost consecrated her virginity to Our Lord, and who from pure choice and an ardent desire to please God, embraced that state so perfectly in itself and so sublime that God the Son himself thought he could not better express its merit than by comparing it to that of the angels in heaven. . . .

Related closely to the high opinion of the priests regarding her virginity was the praise they had for her active prayer life. Father Cholenec detailed that she rarely prayed with her lips moving. Instead, she prayed, as he put it, with her heart and her eyes. Her eyes were filled with tears, and her heart expressed itself in audible sighs: "She appeared immobile and closed up within herself. Through such eagerness to unite herself to God in her prayers, she attained, without any other teacher than the Holy Ghost, a sublime gift of prayer, together with such heavenly sweetness that she often passed several hours at a time in these intimate communications with her God."

Not everyone in the village or in the mission was capable of recognizing the true horizons of her spirituality, and not everyone was capable of steering her in the right direction. For this reason, Kateri's patience and her untiring efforts to incorporate the various spiritual exercises into her daily life become even more remarkable. The fact that her true vocation was well beyond the understanding of her contemporaries in the wilderness added suffering to her in many ways, but she never turned away from it, never complained, and attempted to find her way to her own spiritual destiny.

Kateri had entered the fourth landscape of her existence, the domain of the spirit, where union with God assumes a lustrous beauty, an intimacy, and a vibrancy that makes everything else in the world pale and fade. Baptism was a specific grace for her soul, but it was also a formalizing of the process that had been taking place deep within her all along. The sacrament welcomed her with an even greater urgency to the Divine Embrace.

Actually, Kateri was imitating her namesake, Catherine of Siena, who was a true mystic and contemplative. The Church, in canonizing Catherine and others of her nature, declares that there are many paths to prayerful union with God. The various religious congregations and orders within the Church have been established with the same realization in mind, to provide adequate and prudent frameworks upon which men and women can work toward their own perfection according to the promptings of the Holy Spirit.

The Jesuit priests and the other missionaries in the American wilds gave evidence of the "way of light," the active apostolate that is most common to Christians. While on earth, Jesus Christ was very explicit about the ways in which his followers could imitate him: through the practice of the virtues, through good works, and through love. Most human beings who take being Christian seriously make some attempt to lead virtuous and exemplary lives, distinguished by charity, by compassion, and by a prudent perception of the world and its mad vanities.

The religious congregations and orders that traditionally have trained men and women for work in the missions, in hospitals, schools, sanitariums, chapels, social services, communications, and in countless other institutions that offer the weak or the afflicted genuine care, are based on the Christian ideals of unstinting devotion to Christ and of generosity to Christ's own, the family of mankind. Such a path is difficult, as the demands of caring, of tending to the ill or abused, and of all those activities designed to combat the illusions of the world, exhaust bodies and spirits. Maintaining the Christian spirit of joy amid submission, of kindness in the heat of persecution, charity in the torments of martyrdom, involve the highest faculties of fidelity, honor, and courage. Above all, the active apostolate demands an unstinting awareness of the lures of the world and the failings of other human beings. The many saints of the past have given remarkable testimony to the variety of ways in which true sons and daughters of the Church can aid the world.

There is another path, however, called the "way of darkness." It is the path of prayer, but not the type of prayer that most men and women experience in their lifetimes. It is the mystical road, the way of love and union. It is the road of contemplation. Contemplation as experienced by people in this spiritual world can be translated simply as meaning "the joyful gaze of the soul upon God."

The use of the word "darkness" in this particular form of spiritual advancement does not indicate evil, shadows, or abyssal blindness. The dark path is called that because human beings who are called to the mystical life enter a realm of the spirit in which their senses are not reliable guides as they move toward their spiritual goals. The missionary, for example, can tell by the reception of the faith how well he is serving Christ and the people. He can number converts, witness changes in behavior, can even count the missions that he establishes in the wilderness. The monks and nuns in the great contemplative monasteries and convents, called by many the Church's "treasuries of grace," support the missionary with their sacrifices, their penances, and their prayers. But they never see the results personally. They do not admit converts or establish great mission houses in the wilds. Nothing is visible to them, but they persevere, knowing only that they are called to this form of worship and to this manner of bringing graces to mankind. This is why, for example, Saint Thérèse of Lisieux is honored as a patroness of the Catholic missions. At first look, such a title makes little practical sense. She was a young French girl who lived the last years of her brief life as a nun in a French cloister, seemingly shut away from the rest of the world. And yet the Little Flower is ranked among the patrons of the missions for the Church. Why? Because her prayers and those of others in the religious life and also among the laity provide powerful spiritual gifts and support for the mission labors of the Church and for the spiritual benefit of all Christians everywhere.

Although some mystics were well known in their day, for example, men and women such as Saint John of the Cross and Saint Teresa of Ávila, many of them work out their own apostolate of praise and prayer quite hidden and unappreciated. When Saint Thérèse died, for example, some of her Carmelite Sisters asked what there was to write about her life. They had lived with her as she endured her own agonies of the spirit, had shared meals and prayers with her as she ascended into the heights of mystical union, but they had not understood what was taking place. The mystical souls of this world most often appear as the gentlest, the most docile, the sweetest of all.

The mystics have stepped beyond the usual human experience. For instance, every human being on earth desires companionship, fulfillment in love, commitment to the highest degree, and union with someone who can be all things to his or her life. Marriage provides considerable companionship, fulfillment, commitment, and union, but even in the happiest stages of wedded bliss humans still feel drawn to something well beyond the intimacies of flesh and the visible personality. The spiritual side of men and women yearns for oblation, for the simple act of being in the presence of the One. The world, friends, honors, career accomplishments, even loved ones cannot provide what the spiritual nature of human beings seeks as the natural domain of the soul.

Contemplatives and mystics, those who are gifted by grace with "the joyful gaze of the soul upon God," by instinct are drawn to move beyond the flesh and the realm of the senses. They have a different vision about the world, a rather special understanding. A contemplative is able to rise above the world to see it in its entirety and in its finished form. It is like a person looking down upon an exquisite tapestry. From below, the stitches, the mistakes, the knots of fabric and threads are all exposed. The work is complete, but it is not clear from this angle. From above, however, where the master craftsman has created a pattern of vibrancy and color, of flowing form and style, the tapestry assumes a fascinating identity of its own, imprinted with beauty and charm. The contemplatives of this world, the mystics, see the completed pattern or at least understand the manner in which God is moving and forming all things for the good of souls, no longer caring about mistakes, stitches, or knotted fabrics or threads.

This awareness is centered on the recognition of the presence of God, a spiritual insight that has been the foundation of many saintly lives. Such recognition naturally alters the contemplative's perception of the world and the individual. Each event, each person's honors, sufferings, and death become blended in the pattern that God has allowed, and living within the framework of such a unified whole gives the mystic a unique vision of temporal affairs. At the same time, coming closer to God, a mystic normally develops an acute consciousness of unworthiness, of true wretchedness when compared with the Divine. For this reason mystics are given to great penances, to lives concerned with merit, sacrifice, atonement, and reparation.

As we have seen with Saint Thérèse, the great contemplative religious communities, while providing a monastic setting for the perfecting of human souls, have long been considered harsh and austere. The religious within their walls have taken upon themselves strict diets, limited conversations, simple clothing, labors, prayers, and reparations. Not afraid to be alone with the Alone, these religious pursue their vocations in giving praise, in repenting for themselves and others, and in moving toward the loss of self in the embrace of the Divine. Outsiders who are privileged to visit such monasteries and convents, however, discover that these "austere" religious are normally cheerful, happy, and emotionally balanced in the performance of their daily routines. They display the "sweet docility" that Kateri made evident always.

Long before baptism and acceptance into the Catholic community, Kateri Tekakwitha had discerned the presence of God in her life. She needed no monastic structure to make this evident. She needed no counsel in order to recognize the embrace of the Alone. Her conversion only deepened her spirit and allowed the flowering of true graces in her soul. Had she been in a convent, behind the walls and instructed by the religious who were trained in the mystical life, she would have matured as rapidly, but her role would have been altered. She was the Lily of the Mohawks, the Mystic of the Wilderness, and it was her destiny to attain her spiritual heights in the dense forests of the land.

Immediately after her baptism, the floodgates of her soul opened, and she began to seek more and more solitude and to take on extended periods of prayer. The union with the One had begun, and she was experiencing a rapturous encounter at last. This did not make her particularly popular in the village.

Perhaps her uncle and her other relatives had hoped that by becoming a Christian she would settle some problem within her and would become more involved in village life. They had no way of knowing that more and more she was shocked by what she saw around her, saddened by the brutality and the paganism, and alienated by the mindless pursuit of the flesh.

In her last years, Kateri began to demonstrate clear signs of what the Church calls the "unitive" way. She knelt motionless, totally immersed in prayer in the chapel or in the snow beside the giant cross on the riverbank. She was in communion with God wherever her routine took her, and her rapture was evident on her face. The Native Americans who lived among her noticed the changes as well. She was among them, but her soul was already transfixed, altered by Divine Love. The truly holy in the world display this sort of mystical communion in the way they walk, in the way they talk, and in the way that they greet all things as part of the Divine Plan.

Such an individual confounds the world, especially if she is raised up by God in the wilderness, in an age that does not afford her or her people the sort of consideration that they are owed. The four landscapes of Kateri's existence had blended to form a perfect human, a whole being who was able to offer God praise, thanksgiving, and atonement. She was prepared for her death, as she was prepared to work as God's servant beyond the grave.

In this aspect, Kateri's role in American history becomes ever more defined. Many religious, sincere and faithful, work toward contemplation, toward "the joyful gaze of the soul upon God," but it is not something that can be earned. The mystical grace, the sense and compelling force of unity with the Divine, comes unrequested, unsought. God chooses his mystics, his contemplatives, his enraptured souls. He moves in them, he guides and molds and opens the spirit toward the final embrace, the consuming fire that some great saints have described in the past. No one can ignite that fire personally, no one can carry a torch into the landscape of the mystic. It is God's gift, and the result of grace in a uniquely ordained manner. The fact is that Almighty God chose Kateri Tekakwitha, as he chose Saint Rose of Lima in the Southern Hemisphere. Kateri was not aware of her major role in the history of the Native Americans, although she had a predisposition to understanding that her life would not end in the grave — not in the usual sense of hoping for salvation, resurrection, and life everlasting, but in the manner of continuing as God's servant in the world even when her life's breath had faded.

CHAPTER NINE

SAINT KATERI'S SPIRITUAL LEGACY

Here at the Sault, one may see, in the person of Kateri Tekakwitha, the first Christian virgin which the Iroquois nation has given to the Church of Jesus Christ. God has permitted many wonders to take place at the tomb of this marvelous girl.

Bishop Jean-Baptiste de Saint-Vallier, 1688

The coffin and the rituals of the funeral were designed especially for Kateri, as Native Americans, even in the mission, normally kept to their traditional burial rites. With their sense of oneness with the earth, Indians did not go to great lengths to protect the body from natural decay. Most were wrapped in blankets or in some other prepared shroud and placed gently in the earth. Kateri, however, was to be placed in a coffin, so all could visit her gravesite.

Kateri's final resting place was the source of some disagreement among the priests. Father Chauchetière wanted her to be buried in the mission church cemetery. This was opposed by Father Cholenec, who preferred she be put to rest in the community cemetery. As he was the senior priest, Father Cholenec settled the matter, and Kateri was interred in the community cemetery. As it happened, Kateri had predicted the exact spot of her burial, pointing it out one day to her friends while they were digging the grave of a child. Father Cholenec, however, was not aware of the event and was told of Kateri's prediction only several years after her death.

She was placed with love and care into the coffin that had been carved by the French colonists as a final gift. The coffin was left open for a time to give everyone in the mission a chance to see her and say goodbye. The burial was a mixture of sadness and intense joy, with all the mission population in attendance, some quite inconsolable. They had lost her, but they knew that they would see her again, and proclaimed that she was already in heaven and would be praying for those still on earth.

Word of her death swept beyond the mission compound, of course, carried by the two awed Frenchmen and others. The same phrase was always used when relaying the sad tale: "The saint is dead." No one needed to hear her name, as those words told everyone who was meant. She had been called "the Christian" in her Mohawk village; so she was called "the saint" at Sault. Other Indians and whites from Ville-Marie and elsewhere began arriving unbidden at the mission as soon as the news of Kateri's death spread, and the priests watched as hundreds knelt before the grave and prayed or wept.

The following Friday, which happened to be Good Friday, was again marked by expressions of grief by all the members of the community. The Indian converts cried severely, and they pledged to lead their lives with the same love of Christ and virtue that Kateri had displayed. A group of the Indians then formed the "Followers of Katharine," dedicating themselves to penances and offering up their prayers for those in need of them. Such was the devotion to the memory of Kateri that the number of pilgrims making their way to the graveside grew to such an extent that the Jesuits decided many years later to move Kateri's remains to the mission church cemetery.

The reputation for holiness that had grown in the last years of her life continued in the time after her death.

The Jesuits were well aware of the immense esteem in which Kateri was held by the Native Americans, especially those drawn to the faith by her shining example. In their preaching and in their lessons, they held her up as an example of holiness and the perfection of the virtues. Father Chauchetière used images of her in his teachings, including a large painting that he held up to show Indian converts that she was a model for them in developing their love of Christ.

In the annual accounting of the mission dated 1680, the year of Kateri's death, Father Frémin expressed his gratitude to her for being a model to the Indian converts, then added that even in death the honor paid to her had grown and that her reputation as a saint was spreading rapidly across New France. Within a few months, in fact, Kateri was being called the "Protectress of Canada" among the faithful. In 1688, Bishop de Saint-Vallier, who had visited the Sault Mission and had been so edified by the Christian community there, stated:

Here at the Sault, one may see, in the person of Kateri

Tekakwitha, the first Christian virgin which the Iroquois nation has given to the Church of Jesus Christ. God has permitted many wonders to take place at the tomb of this marvelous girl.

She was also honored as the "Genevieve of New France," the "Protectress" of the mission, and the "First Virgin of the Iroquois." The story of her life and virtues soon passed across the Atlantic. Father Frémin had sailed to France and talked about her, but she was already being discussed by other French Jesuits and by French colonists who told their friends and family about this extraordinary young woman. Inevitably, the accounts reached the royal court of the Sun King, Louis XIV.

Adding to her reputation for holiness were the multiplying numbers of wonders and apparitions being reported by Native Americans, French colonists, and the priests themselves.

Father Chauchetière was the first to see Kateri. Six days after she was buried, he was working in the church and looked up to see her standing beside him. Radiant, smiling, and emanating pure joy, she was accompanied by two other images: a church turned upside down and a Native American tied to a flaming stake. The priest, shocked and shaken, watched in silence for several hours, trying to understand what Kateri was telling him. Three years later, he and everyone else understood her message, as it was carried out by two terrible events. A tornado struck the village during a frightful storm, and the church was lifted from the ground, swirled in the air, and then set on the earth again, upside down. Three priests were inside the church when it happened, but when the structure fell to the ground and shattered, they were discovered bruised but generally unharmed. The second image had foretold a more dreadful event, which came about when the Onondagas attacked the mission during a period of intertribal warfare in 1683. An Iroquois Christian was taken captive, and the Onondagas burned him alive. They reported later that the man died in agony, but without cursing them or wailing to be set free. Even in his last torments he exhorted them to accept Christ and to take on the freedom, the wholeness, the beauty of the faith in their lives.

Anastasia was the second person to see her after her death. Early one morning, while she was sleeping, she heard Kateri's voice beside her bed. "Mother," the young woman called, "open your eyes and look at me." When she looked at the vision, Anastasia saw a radiant and lovely Kateri standing before her holding a shining cross. Kateri said that she had loved the cross while on earth and loved it even more in paradise. This visit was taken by Anastasia to be warning and a gift — a warning that Anastasia needed to prepare herself for the cross that was coming. And, indeed, the cross arrived. Three of her children were killed in war in the coming years.

Marie Theresa, who had felt the loss of Kateri perhaps more than anyone else, reported that Kateri appeared to her one day to chide her about a particular fault and to encourage her to redouble her efforts and look to heaven. She started a group called the Sisters of Kateri, and was joined by several other young Indian converts. They lived semireligious lives, maintaining the standards of perfection and purity that Kateri had exemplified in her lifetime.

Father Chauchetière, however, was to be visited yet again.

When he found himself in the company of Kateri a second time, she asked him to paint her portrait to inspire her people to accept the Catholic faith. He was troubled by the vision, naturally. He started the portrait, stopped, and then began again. Apparently it was a rather strange picture when completed, as Father Cholenec referred to it in the records as "somewhat original." But that portrait worked a miracle instantly, and the local populace began to clamor for more pictures. Father Chauchetière drew or painted Kateri every day.

Stories of healings began almost immediately after her death and became even more numerous as the pilgrims to her grave began to arrive at the Sault Mission. One of the most intense accounts was sent to Father Cholenec in 1696 by Father Pierre Rémy, a French Sulpician who served in the mission at Lachine, near Montréal.

Father Rémy began the letter by admitting that he was initially incredulous about the stories being told of Kateri's intercession, until he was himself cured of deafness in his right ear. He asked for her intercession before saying a Mass, and his hearing began to improve by the end of Communion. By the conclusion of the Mass his hearing had been completely restored. He next thanked her for her intercession in recovering from an inflammation of sciatica and from severe rheumatism in his right arm. Such was his confidence in her that he took to instructing his parishioners to ask for her aid first when encountering a problem in their lives, especially infirmities.

He devoted the most important part of his account, however, to the more than thirty claims of cures, healings, and intercessions that took place after individuals implored her intercession. The cures were of children and adults and included a thirteen-month-old boy dying from convulsions, to a five-year-old girl with incurable scrofula (a severe skin disease), to a two-year-old boy dying of consumption. Father Rémy was an eyewitness to most of the cases and placed his name in the testimony. He likewise did his best to gather information from his parishioners in order for his account to be as reliable as possible.

In the letter from Father Cholenec to the Jesuit Father Le Blanc in 1715, the priest wrote that he was composing a brief life of Kateri because of the marvels that were being attributed to her intercession on an almost daily basis. As one of the priests who cared for her soul, Father Cholenec had been an eyewitness to the holiness of her life, but he was also a witness to her miracles in the years after her passing. He discussed in the letter the fact that she was a beloved and holy figure among the Native Americans and also among the French at Montréal and Québec, who regularly made pilgrimages to her grave. Many of the pilgrims came, he added, out of gratitude for her intercession in some illness or for a miraculous cure.

Father Cholenec included the testimony of two significant leaders in New France. The first was Father Joseph de la Colombière, the canon of the Cathedral at Québec. He suffered for months with chronic dysentery and other ailments, and in desperation turned to Kateri. He promised to make a pilgrimage to her grave, and almost immediately found his medical problems easing, whereupon he set out for the mission. By the time he was on the road, he was completely cured.

The second was Monsieur du Lhut, a captain of the French

Marine Corps and the commander of Fort Frontenac. In a signed affidavit, he testified that after suffering for twenty-three years with untreatable gout, he asked Kateri for her assistance and promised to go to her grave at the mission should he be healed. He was almost immediately cured and, being faithful to his pledge, made his way to her burial place.

In another 1715 letter, Father Cholenec wrote to Father Michael Angelo Tamburini, the General of the Society of Jesus, about Kateri. He once again insisted that she be better known for her holiness and called her "a new star in the New World." Within a few months of her death, Father Cholenec told him, she was being credited with miracles all over Canada, and small items from her life were being held devoutly as relics and were the source of spiritual encouragement. The sick and the lame were being brought to her grave, where they were healed.

Other accounts stated that novenas and prayers, the touch of one of her moccasins or crosses, even the thought of Kateri, was all that was necessary for human beings to be relieved of their physical sufferings.

Because of the overwhelming powers of Kateri to aid those she had left behind, she was called the "Thaumaturge," the healer of the New World. The cures were recorded by authorities as they happened.

Even Hot Cinders benefited from the young woman he had aided so many years before. The chief's wife was terribly ill and in danger of dying when Kateri's coverlet was brought to her bed. She was wrapped in the coverlet and was cured instantly.

Finally, Claude-Charles La Roy, Sieur de Bacqueville de

la Potherie, an adventurer and official in New France, published his memoirs in 1716 and included an account of Kateri, including her reputation for holiness and her cures. Aware of Kateri's fame for her goodness and her impact on the whole of New France, de la Potherie composed a verse in her honor:

De ta grace, Seigneur, a lumière eternelle
Éclaire, quand tu veux, change choisit, appelle
Les plus sauvages coeurs et les attaché à toi;

Ainsi l'on voit passer par elle
Celui d'une Iroquoise animé, pleine du zèle,
De la nuit de l'erreur au grand jour de la Foi.

[Of your grace, Lord, eternal light
Lights, when you want, change when choosing,
Wildest hearts and attached to you;

Thus we see through it
That of an Iroquois lively, full of zeal,
The night of the error to light of the Faith.]

CHAPTER TEN

SAINT KATERI'S BEATIFICATION AND CANONIZATION

Kateri Tekakwitha, the "Lily of the Mohawks," the Iroquois maiden, who in seventeenth-century North America was the first to renew the marvels of sanctity of Saint Scholastica, Saint Gertrude, Saint Catherine of Siena, Saint Angela Merici, and Saint Rose of Lima, preceding, along the path of Love, her great spiritual sister: Thérèse of the Child Jesus.

Pope Blessed John Paul II to Native Americans, 1987

Within four years of Kateri's passing, the decision was made to move her relics from the cemetery in the mission to the mission church cemetery. This was largely because of the number of pilgrims who were visiting her burial place, but also because Father Chauchetière deemed it appropriate that she should be given a place of honor in the new church that had been built after the storm had destroyed the old church a year earlier, as Kateri had predicted. Over the next decades, as the fortunes of New France and the missions were caught up in the bitter struggle between France and England, the mission church had to be moved four times.

Each time, the relics of Kateri were taken with great reverence by the community, the only remains to be so revered. Ultimately, they were put to rest at the mission at Kahnawake (modern Caughnawaga), at a mission founded in 1719, in a case made of ebony. At the same time, her relics, parts of her remains, were distributed to other Native American mission outposts.

The place of her burial was marked by a cross. By the 1840s, owing to the long years in which the French were blocked from sending Jesuits or missionaries into English-controlled territory, the cross had fallen down and had not been replaced. In May 1842, however, the Jesuits were finally allowed to return to Canada. On July 23, 1843, on the seventh Sunday after Pentecost, they celebrated the restoration of the cross, and the Jesuit priest Father Joseph Marcoux, the pastor of Caughnawaga, was allowed to place some of Kateri's relics in the new monument. Father Rémy Joseph Tellier wrote an account of the ceremony in a letter sent the next year to the provincial in France. The new cross was twenty-five feet tall, made of wood, and had been carved by three residents. Some fragments of bone were encased in the hollow of the trunk. Beneath four banners decorated with French and Iroquois inscriptions, a large crowd gathered along the bank of the Portage River. On the right was a gathering of Iroquois, including chiefs and a maiden named Tegahkouita, who carried a painting of her namesake. To the left was a crowd of French-Canadians and English from across the region. Cannons were then drawn to the site and used to mark each moment of the ceremony. With the first blast of the cannons, the solemn procession of the missionaries walked from a nearby house to the cross. Hymns were sung, and a Father Martin delivered a homily in French. The Iroquois performed their own songs and music, the first time in a century and a half that their music had been heard in the area. Father Marcoux then delivered a sermon in Iroquois (the priest was fluent in the tongue and had even composed a dictionary in Iroquois-French and French-Iroquois). A third sermon was given in English by a Father Hudon, who performed the formal blessing of the cross, which was then elevated and installed as the cannons gave off a final volley. Kateri's relics remained in the cross until 1888, when they were enshrined in a new marble monument.

~ ~ ~

The excitement that surrounded the restoration of the cross in 1843 raised two obvious questions. The first was why there was no active effort promoting the cause for canonization for Kateri; the second was why, despite her obvious reputation for holiness, a cause had not been launched long before.

These questions were taken up in the *positio* for the cause that was submitted to Rome in 1938 in the hopes that the Holy See might recognize Kateri's heroic virtues. In his remarkable introduction to the *positio*, the relator general of the cause, Franciscan Father F. Antonelli, observed that a precise series of historical circumstances had created long and insuperable delays in starting her cause for canonization. He began by noting that the location of the Mission of Sault Saint Francis Xavier, where virtually all the pertinent events in the life of Kateri took place, was not a permanent site and had been moved repeatedly over the years until finally settling at Caughnawaga, Canada, in 1719.

He then pointed out the fact that the ecclesiastical structure of the Church in Canada was long unsettled. This is demonstrated by the defeat of France in the French and Indian War in 1759 and the final ceding of Canada to England in the Treaty of Paris of 1763. The war and the treaty ended New France and marked the beginning of a long period in which the Church across Canada was directed by only the Diocese of Québec. This state of affairs changed only in 1836, and in the intervening years the missions had been rendered all but dormant, and Catholics faced varying degrees of hostility on the part of the government.

Finally, there was the tortured history of the Society of Jesus. The missions of Canada were entrusted to the Jesuits, including all those that were connected to Kateri's life. The Society suffered immediately with the defeat of France in 1759 as the English moved to prevent any more Jesuits from coming to Canada to serve in the missions. The number of Jesuits in Canada declined swiftly, so that by 1763 and the official handover of New France there were barely twenty Jesuits in the colony. Within a decade, there were only eleven. That dark year of 1773 brought the formal suppression of the Jesuit order by Pope Clement XIV, under intense pressure from the rulers of Europe, who hated their learning and especially their commitment to the papacy.

With the suppression, the English confiscated all Jesuit property in what had been New France. The last Jesuit priest in Canada died in Québec in 1800. Not until 1842 were the Jesuits, who had been re-formed in 1814 by Pope Pius VII, allowed back into Canada as missionaries, and only in 1903 were they permitted to take control again of the old Sault Mission.

It was thus not surprising that a cause was never initiated by the proper Church authorities in Canada, especially after the death of New France. Moreover, Kateri was not unique in this. All the other great and heroic figures of Catholicism in Canada had their causes delayed for precisely the same reasons: Marie Guyart, who died in 1672, but whose cause was started only in 1877; Marguerite Bourgeoys, who died in 1700, but whose cause began in 1878; and the Jesuit North American Martyrs, who died in the mid-seventeenth century, but whose cause was initiated only in 1916.

With the return of the Jesuits to Canada's missions in 1842, the love and respect for Kateri were found to be very much alive in the hearts of Native American Catholics and many Canadians and even Americans.

The first great effort to start a cause for canonization for Kateri came, in fact, from the bishops of the United States. In 1884, during the Third Plenary Council of Baltimore, Jesuit Fathers asked the bishops of the United States to give their support to a petition that was to be sent to Pope Leo XIII, asking that causes for canonization be introduced for the two Jesuit martyrs, René Goupil and Isaac Jogues, and for Kateri Tekakwitha. The petition was formally presented to the bishops during the seventh session and was signed by all the members. It was sent to Pope Leo XIII on December 6, 1884, by Cardinal James Gibbons, archbishop of Baltimore. The petition read:

Most Holy Father:

By the disposition of Divine Providence it has come to pass that in recent years attention has been drawn again to that part of the Diocese of Albany which in the seventeenth century was made illustrious by the virtues and martyrdom of three Christians. Of these one was René Goupil . . . felled by a blow of the tomahawk . . . September 29, 1642. . . . Father Isaac Jogues immediately followed him . . . he was tomahawked by the Iroquois, October 18, 1646.

To these is added the Iroquois virgin Katherine Tekakwitha who was born in the very place at which the above Servants of God shed their blood. While she was yet a young girl, in order to practice the Christian faith and perform her exercises of piety more freely, she went, along with some other Christian Iroquois to a village in Canada which is now known as Caughnawaga. There she gave evidence of her innocence of life and that she was a splendid example of every virtue, until in the twenty-fourth year of her age she very piously died in the Lord, in 1680, leaving behind her a renown for sanctity which has been confirmed by wonderful events.

Thus the names of René Goupil, Father Isaac Jogues and Katharine Tekakwitha have been accepted among the faithful of the United States and in the Dominion of Canada as most renowned, and in an uninterrupted tradition have appeared in both civil and ecclesiastical history. Several publications — whether monographs or biographies — have appeared in their especial praise. Not a few contemporary documents are preserved in archives — these confirm full faith in the published narratives.

Accordingly, after having deeply considered this matter, we humbly beg of Your Holiness that the cause of beatification of René Goupil, Father Isaac Jogues and Katharine Tekakwitha be introduced by authority of the Holy See. Such a cause will inspire the devotion of the faithful of this country by new examples drawn from their very midst; it will promote zeal with a new stimulus for the conversion of the Indians; it will encourage the Indians themselves to embrace the Christian faith because of the honors bestowed upon one of their fellow tribesmen; it will add new protectors to our country and afford it native patrons.

> James Gibbons,
> Archbishop of Baltimore and
> Apostolic Delegate
> In his own name and in the
> name of the other prelates met
> in the Third Plenary Council
> December 6, 1884

The next year, additional petitions were sent to the Holy See by more than twenty-five Native American Catholic communities across the United States and Canada. Two were especially notable, as they came from the Indians at the Caughnawaga Mission in Canada in 1885, which was then under the direction of the Oblates of Mary Immaculate. They were sent in Latin, and named René Goupil, Isaac Jogues, and Kateri:

Holy Father, Sovereign Pontiff

We, the undersigned inhabitants of the village known as Caughnawaga, venerate you with all our heart, as minister of the word of God and of our higher life.

This is our reason for writing to you: We have heard that the American bishops, recently assembled in the City of Baltimore, have prayed you to declare that Katharine Tekakwitha, who died two hundred years ago in our village, is dwelling as Blessed among the number of those who are in heaven.

Illustrious were her deeds when living, and it is certain that after her death she healed many sick.

We shall exult with great joy, our Holy Father, if you agree that we may venerate and invoke her in our church in the same way that other saints, whom the Church honors, are invoked. We hope by this for an increase of religion in our village: that young people, emulating the example of Katharine, will be careful not to be stained by sin, and that many Indians who have not yet joined the Catholic Church may enter its fold.

There are two others who though Frenchmen are still for us as if they were our own, because they taught our ancestors the Sign of the Cross and the way of salvation, and were therefore put to death by the wicked. These two also we should like to hold in veneration as our protectors, our advocates. Their names are Father Isaac Jogues and Brother René Goupil.

If you will kindly favor us with these three as patrons, it will make our hearts happy, our conduct good, and our children will grow up perfect; many Indian people not yet baptized will enter the Catholic Church and realize the glory of heaven.

Our Father the Pope:

Though we Indians are very poor and miserable, yet our Maker had great pity on us and gave us the Catholic religion. Moreover, he had pity on us again and gave us Katharine Tekakwitha. This holy virgin, an Indian like ourselves, being favored by Jesus Christ with a great grace, grew up very good, had a great love for our Maker, and died good and holy, and is now glorious in heaven, as we believe, and prays for us all. This virgin, we believe, was given to us from God as a great favor, for she is our little sister. But now we hope that thou, our Father, who art the Vicar of Jesus Christ, wilt grant us a favor likewise; we beg thee with all our hearts to speak and say: "You Indians, my children, take Katharine as an object of your veneration in the Church, because she is holy and is in heaven."

There are also two others, though Frenchmen, yet are as if they were Indians, because they taught the Indians the Sign of the Cross and the way to heaven; and for this they were killed by bad Indians. Their names are Black Robe Isaac Jogues and Brother René Goupil. We wish to have these two also as objects of our veneration, as our protectors and our advocates.

If thou givest us these three as our patrons, our hearts will be glad, our behavior will be good, and our children will become perfect; also a great many unbaptized Indians will enter into the Catholic Church and will see the glory of heaven.

Priority was given in the next years to the cause of the North American Martyrs. After their cause was opened in 1916, they were canonized in 1930 by Pope Pius IX. The next year, the Diocese of Albany officially began its own process of investigation into the life and possible heroic virtue of Kateri. The petition for the opening of the cause was sent to Rome and the case was given its official start on July 11, 1932. Six years later, the *positio* for the cause was submitted to authorities in the Congregation for the Causes of Saints, with the intention of demonstrating the heroic virtue of Kateri. The *positio* was accepted, and on January 3, 1943, Pope Pius XII declared Kateri venerable.

Kateri's cause for canonization proceeded over the next years, guided by the prayers of Native American Catholics and the labors of those involved in her cause, in particular Monsignor Paul A. Lenz, the vice-postulator and head of the Bureau of Catholic Indian Missions and the Jesuit priest Paolo Molinari. In 1980, Pope John Paul II gave his permission for the miracles that took place after Kateri's death, as attested to at the time, to be considered suitable testimony for her beatification. After intensive study, the Holy See delivered the joyous news to Native Americans across the United States and Canada that Kateri Tekakwitha would be declared blessed, the final stage before canonization. She was beatified in Rome on June 22, 1980, by Pope Blessed John Paul II, with several others: an Italian Jesuit, Giuseppe de Anchieta; Pietro de San José Betancur, a Third Order Franciscan; and two Canadian figures, Marie Guyart of the Incarnation; and François de Montmorency Laval, the bishop of Québec. Kateri's feast day was set on April 17, but in the United States her feast day is July 14. Pope John Paul declared about Kateri:

This wonderful crown of new blesseds, God's bountiful gift to his Church, is completed by the sweet, frail yet strong figure of a young woman who died when she was only twenty-four years old: Kateri Tekakwitha, the "Lily of the Mohawks," the Iroquois maiden, who in seventeenth-century North America was the first to renew the marvels of sanctity of Saint Scholastica, Saint Gertrude, Saint Catherine of Siena, Saint Angela Merici and Saint Rose of Lima, preceding, along the path of Love, her great spiritual sister: Thérèse of the Child Jesus.

She spent her short life partly in what is now the State of New York and partly in Canada. She is a kind, gentle and hardworking person, spending her time working, praying, and meditating. At the age of twenty she receives baptism. Even when following her tribe in the hunting seasons, she continues her devotions, before a rough cross carved by herself in the forest. When her family urges her to marry, she replies very serenely and calmly that she has Jesus as her only spouse. This decision, in view of the social conditions of women in the Indian tribes at the time, exposes Kateri to the risk of living as an outcast and in poverty. It is a bold, unusual and prophetic gesture: on 25 March 1679, at the age of twenty-three, with the consent of her spiritual director, Kateri takes a vow of perpetual virginity, as far as we know the first time that this was done among the North American Indians.

The last months of her life are an ever clearer manifestation of her solid faith, straightforward humility, calm resignation, and radiant joy, even in the midst of terrible sufferings. Her fast words, simple and sublime, whispered at the moment of death, sum up, like a noble hymn, a life of purest charity: "Jesus, I love you . . . "

With Kateri's beatification, Native American Catholics and Catholics all over the world took part in celebrations and continued to work toward making her better known and promoting her cause. A prayer for the canonization of Kateri Tekakwitha was approved and distributed widely. It reads:

> O God, who, among the many marvels of your grace in the New World, did cause to blossom on the banks of the Mohawk and of the Saint Lawrence, the pure and tender Lily, Kateri Tekakwitha, grant we beseech you, the favor we beg through her intercession; that this young lover of Jesus and of his Cross may soon be counted among her saints by Holy Mother Church, and that our hearts may be enkindled with a stronger desire to imitate her innocence and faith. Through the same Christ our Lord. Amen.

Kateri is also given honor in two national shrines in the United States: the National Shrine of Blessed Kateri Tekak- witha in Fonda, New York, and the Shrine of Our Lady of Martyrs in Auriesville, New York. She is also commemorated at the Basilica of the National Shrine of the Immaculate Concep- tion in Washington, D.C. There are also the active and dedicat- ed organizations and apostolates devoted to promoting Kateri's cause and providing pastoral assistance to Native Americans in her name, such as the Tekakwitha League and the National Tekakwitha Conference, which publish newsletters, books, and articles, and welcome inquiries and reports of Kateri's intercessions. The Tekakwitha Conference, based in Great Falls, Montana, was started in 1939 to bring together Native American Catholics from across the many tribes in the United States.

~ ~ ~

The final step in the canonization of Kateri was the acceptance of a miracle by the Congregation for the Causes of Saints in Rome. Although a number of cases were presented over the years, none was able to meet the congregation's very stringent requirements for approval. That all changed with the possible miracle that took place in 2006. A six-year-old Native American boy, Jacob "Jake" Finkbonner of Ferndale, Washington, cut his lip when he hit the base of the hoop while playing basketball. An aggressive bacteria, streptococcus A, entered Jake's bloodstream through the injury, and the boy was stricken with necrotizing fasciitis, a rare but deadly form of flesh-eating bacterial infection. Despite the efforts of doctors to prevent the spread of the bacteria, the child continued to decline, and a priest was summoned to give him the last rites. The priest, Father Tim Sauer, suggested that the family pray to God through the intercession of Blessed Kateri, especially as Jake's father is Native American, a member of the Lummi tribe. In addition to her place of honor in the faith lives of Native Americans, the priest was also aware that Kateri had been disfigured by smallpox, making it even more appropriate to seek her intercession.

Significantly, Sister Kateri Mitchell, S.S.A., a Mohawk nun and executive director of the Tekakwitha Conference, gave a first-class relic of Kateri to the priest, and it was pinned to Jake's pillow by his mother, Elsa. To the surprise of the doctors, Jacob not only survived but the bacteria were gone. Over the next several years, Jake underwent multiple surgeries to repair the disfigurements caused by the bacteria, and the question was raised as whether the healing could be considered a genuine miracle.

Prudently, Vatican officials waited several years to see if the bacteria returned. When it did not, a full inquiry into the potential cure, including both theological and medical experts, was launched. Theological experts concluded that the prayers had indeed been focused on Kateri's intercession; the medical investigation ultimately determined that the remission could not be explained in purely medical terms, as is required for all such prospective miracles. The congregation relied on their expert testimony.

Finally, after determining with moral certainty that a miracle had, indeed, occurred, the officials of the congregation approved the cure of Jacob Finkbonner as the miracle needed for canonization. On December 19, 2011, Pope Benedict XVI accepted the recommendation of the congregation and formally approved the miracle, paving the way for the canonization of Kateri Tekakwitha. On February 18, 2012, the Vatican announced that the date had been set for the canonization: October 21, 2012. On the same day, Pope Benedict XVI would canonize several other saints, including Blessed Marianne Cope, a Franciscan Sister of Syracuse who served the lepers on Molokai and provided vital leadership at the leper colony of Kalaupapa in the years after Saint Damien de Veuster's death in 1888.

On April 21, 2012, Pope Benedict XVI spoke about both

Kateri and Marianne Cope when addressing the Papal Foundation, benefactors of the Holy See from the United States:

> In coming months I will have the honor of canonizing two new saints from North America. Blessed Kateri Tekakwitha and Blessed Mother Marianne Cope are striking examples of sanctity and heroic charity, but they also remind us of the historic role played by women in the building up of the Church in America. By their example and intercession, may all of you be confirmed in the pursuit of holiness and in your efforts to contribute to the growth of God's kingdom in the hearts of people today.

Word of the miracle's approval and Kateri's canonization was met with utter joy by Native Americans. Father Wayne C. Paysse, executive director of the Bureau of Catholic Indian Missions, expressed the jubilation in a statement issued immediately after the announcement. Kateri's canonization, it said, would be "one of the first actions of the church during the Year of Faith, which begins next October 11. Surely this is a signal to us that soon-to-be Saint Kateri Tekakwitha is for all the church both a model of faith and of the new evangelization. . . . For now, let us continue to pray to God for all we need, firm in the knowledge that Blessed Kateri is interceding for us from her place in heaven."

In its newsletter for March–April 2012, the Tekakwitha Conference included a Prayer of Thanksgiving:

For the first-class miracle attributed to Blessed Kateri
Tekakwitha approved by our Holy Father on
    December 19, 2011
For all people who have come to know the faith
    journey of Blessed Kateri
For all who have received favors and a reawakening in
    their own faith life through Blessed Kateri
Favors received for health of body, mind and spirit

Psalm 66:1–3
Shout for joy to God, all the earth!
Sing the glory of his name
Make his praise glorious
Say to God: "How awesome are your deeds."

We pray in thanksgiving to our Holy Father Pope
    Benedict XVI for his approval of the first-class
    miracle and the canonization of Kateri
    Tekakwitha, and to Father Paul Molinari, S.J.,
    postulator (Rome), and Monsignor Paul Lenz,
    U.S. vice-postulator (D.C.), for their many hours
    and years of work for the cause of Kateri
    Tekakwitha's sainthood.
With gratitude to the Archdiocese of Seattle,
    Archbishop Brunett, and Bishop Tyson, who

worked with Monsignor Lenz by providing the resources to introduce the case of Jacob Finkbonner (Lummi Nation, Washington) as a potential first-class miracle to the cause of saints in Rome.